Ultimate Modern jQuery for Web App Development

Create Stunning Interactive Web Applications with Seamless DOM Manipulation, Animation, and AJAX Integration of jQuery and JavaScript

Laurence Svekis

www.orangeava.com

First published: March 2024

Published by: Orange Education Pvt Ltd, AVA™

Address: 9, Daryaganj, Delhi, 110002

ISBN: 978-81-97081-94-1

www.orangeava.com

Dedicated To

Alexis and Sebastian Svekis

Thank you for your support

About the Author

Laurence Svekis is an esteemed web developer, online educator, and entrepreneur, distinguished for his dynamic contributions to the field of technology and digital learning. With a career spanning over two decades in developing web applications, he has become a cornerstone in the online educational sphere, teaching programming courses and sharing his extensive knowledge with a global audience.

Laurence's journey in the realm of web development is marked by his early adoption and mastery of various programming languages, including a notable proficiency in JavaScript. His expertise extends into the intricate functionalities of Google Workspace.

As an online instructor, Laurence has authored a plethora of courses that cater to a wide range of topics in web development. These courses are not only comprehensive but are also designed to be accessible to learners at different stages of their coding journey, from beginners to advanced practitioners. His commitment to education is evident in his achievement of reaching over one million students worldwide, a testament to the impact and reach of his teaching methods.

Beyond his online courses, Laurence has also made his mark as a best-selling author. His publications resonate with his teaching philosophy, offering readers practical insights and guiding them through the complexities of web development and programming with clarity and ease.

Laurence's passion for technology and innovation doesn't stop at teaching and writing. He is also an entrepreneur at heart, constantly exploring new frontiers in web technology and developing solutions that address real-world challenges. His enthusiasm for sharing knowledge and empowering others to harness the power of technology underscores his role as a leader and visionary in the digital world.

To sum up, Laurence Svekis stands out as a top-tier web developer, an influential online educator, a best-selling author, and an inspiring entrepreneur. His contributions have not only enriched the field of web development but have also paved the way for countless learners to unlock their potential in the digital landscape.

About the Technical Reviewer

Siddharth Shrivastava is a seasoned Front-End Technical Lead at HCLTech, specializing in crafting accessible and inclusive products, along with digital experiences tailored for the web. His journey in the tech landscape began in 2014, and over the past transformative 9+ years, he has built software for FinTech, Telecom, and Banking clients in the USA.

Siddharth's evolution has led him from crafting websites to mastering dynamic front-end technologies. Currently, at HCL, he orchestrates the conversion of mockups into vibrant interfaces, aligning technological prowess with software life cycles. His work not only exhibits technical expertise but also delivers substantial value to the products of esteemed clients.

Before moving to the USA, Siddharth worked for a FinTech client in India, gaining valuable experience in the FinTech domain and understanding compliance and data-driven development. Prior to that, he worked with a Telecom client, where he migrated the website from Angular to React. Siddharth started his career at Cognizant, working as a full-stack Engineer with C#, JavaScript, and Angular.

Siddharth Shrivastava's story is one of continuous learning, innovation, and dedication to his craft. His work reflects his belief that a problem is an opportunity to do your best, and his commitment to delivering substantial value through his technical expertise.

Acknowledgements

I am deeply grateful to a host of individuals whose expertise, insights, and encouragement were indispensable in the creation of this book. First and foremost, a heartfelt thank you to the jQuery community and everyone involved.

I am also indebted to my fellow educators and students in the web development realm, whose questions and challenges inspired me significantly. Their curiosity and eagerness to learn fueled my motivation to make each chapter, from the basics of jQuery to advanced AJAX methods, both informative and accessible.

Lastly, my children deserve immense gratitude for their unwavering support and patience throughout the countless hours spent in writing and revising. This book is not just a reflection of my knowledge but a testament to the collaborative effort and shared passion for web development that we all hold dear.

Together, we have created a guide that I hope will empower and inspire both new and experienced developers in their journey through the dynamic world of jQuery.

Preface

This book is a concise yet thorough exploration of jQuery, beginning with its basic syntax and how to embed it in HTML files, and extending to advanced topics such as AJAX for dynamic content updates. Each chapter methodically builds on the previous, covering element selection, animation, DOM manipulation, and more, culminating in practical projects that apply what you've learned in real-world contexts.

As we traverse the chapters, readers will gain proficiency in selecting and manipulating page elements, animating web interfaces, and harnessing the full potential of the Document Object Model (DOM) with jQuery's intuitive methods. Practical projects, such as creating a dynamic list with interactive elements, not only reinforce theoretical knowledge but also encourage the application of skills in real-world scenarios

By the end, you'll be adept at using jQuery to craft interactive, responsive web experiences. Embark on this journey to unlock the full potential of web development with jQuery.

Chapter 1. Getting Started with jQuery: Introduces readers to jQuery, its syntax, and the process of adding it to HTML files. By the end of this chapter, you will be well-prepared to use jQuery for creating engaging, interactive web applications and improving your development process. Let's dive into the world of jQuery.

Chapter 2. Selection of Page Elements and DOM Element Selection jQuery: This chapter focuses on mastering the selection and manipulation of page elements and navigating the Document Object Model (DOM). It begins with the fundamental basics of jQuery's Basic Selectors, targeting elements by tags, classes, or IDs. The journey continues through the intricate use of Attribute and Pseudo Selectors for more specific element targeting. Furthermore, it delves into jQuery's traversal techniques for dynamic element manipulation. The chapter concludes with an in-depth look at Filtering Elements, essential for creating complex and responsive web interfaces.

Chapter 3. Element Hide and Show Methods and Animation Effects: This chapter explains how to hide and show elements on a web page using jQuery's built-in methods and how to create animation effects. In the realm of web development, the ability to control visibility and add animation effects to page elements can transform a static website into an interactive and engaging experience. jQuery offers a robust set of methods to achieve this, opening up a world of possibilities for creating dynamic web content. In this chapter, we will explore these methods, from simple hide and show techniques to more advanced fading and sliding effects, equipping you with the skills to breathe life into your web pages.

Chapter 4. Manipulating Element Contents and Inserting Elements: This chapter covers how to manipulate the contents of web page elements using jQuery and how to add new elements to a web page. Dive into the exciting world of manipulating the contents of web page elements and inserting new elements using the power of jQuery. Whether you're a seasoned web developer or just getting started, mastering these techniques will significantly enhance your ability to create dynamic and interactive web pages.

Chapter 5. DOM Manipulation and Selection: This chapter covers how to manipulate and select elements on a web page using jQuery's DOM manipulation methods. Take a deeper dive into the world of Document Object Model (DOM) manipulation and selection using jQuery. Building upon the foundational concepts covered earlier, we will explore advanced techniques to dynamically modify the structure of a web page. By the end of this chapter, you will have a thorough understanding of how to wield jQuery's power to manipulate the DOM effectively.

Chapter 6. jQuery Dynamic List Project - Interactive Elements: This chapter provides a hands-on project that teaches readers how to create a dynamic list with interactive elements using jQuery. Embark on a practical project using jQuery, where we will create a dynamic list with interactive elements. This project will allow readers to apply their knowledge of jQuery to build a real-world, interactive feature that can be used in web applications. Let's dive in!

Chapter 7. CSS Properties and Element Attribute: This chapter explains how to get and set CSS properties and element attributes using jQuery. We will explore how to work with CSS properties and element attributes using jQuery. This knowledge is essential for dynamically modifying the appearance and behavior of web page elements.

Chapter 8. Traversing Page Elements: This chapter covers how to traverse and select page elements using jQuery's traversal methods. We will explore advanced techniques for traversing and selecting page elements using jQuery. These methods will allow readers to navigate the DOM tree efficiently and select specific elements based on their relationships, attributes, and states.

Chapter 9. jQuery Data and Element Index Method: This chapter focuses on two crucial jQuery methods: `data()` and `index()`. These methods play a significant role in enhancing efficiency in manipulating page elements. The data() method is explored for its ability to attach and retrieve custom data to and from elements - a feature particularly useful for storing state information or metadata. The chapter meticulously explains the usage of `data()` for both storing and accessing associated data. Conversely, the `index()` method is presented as a tool for obtaining the index position of an element relative to its siblings, aiding in specific operations within a list or group of elements.

Chapter 10. Handling Events with jQuery: This chapter provides a comprehensive guide to handling events with jQuery, a key element in the development of dynamic web applications. It begins with an overview of the JavaScript event model and then delves into jQuery's capabilities for binding and triggering events. Readers will learn to utilize various jQuery event methods such as `.click()`, `.hover()`, `.submit()`, and `.keypress()` for effective user interaction management. Advanced techniques, including event delegation for dynamically created elements and the use of the `.on()` method for binding multiple events, are also covered.

Chapter 11. Advanced Event Handling Techniques: This chapter delves into advanced event handling techniques in jQuery, emphasizing the efficient use of the `.on()` method for dynamic event management. Through interactive exercises, the chapter guides readers in mastering the intricacies of event attachment, enhancing their ability to create powerful web interactions. Key concepts such as event bubbling and propagation are thoroughly explored, providing clear insights into their significant roles in event behavior.

Chapter 12. jQuery AJAX Methods and Callback Options: This chapter provides a thorough exploration of AJAX methods and callback options in jQuery - a crucial aspect for developing interactive and responsive web applications. AJAX, or Asynchronous JavaScript and XML, enables updating web content without full page reloads, enhancing user experience with swift responsiveness. The cornerstone of jQuery's AJAX functionality is the `$.ajax()` method, which facilitates making HTTP requests and handling server responses.

Get a Free eBook

We hope you are enjoying your recently purchased book! Your feedback is incredibly valuable to us, and to all other readers looking for great books.

If you found this book helpful or enjoyable, we would truly appreciate it, if you could take a moment to leave a short review with a 5 star rating on Amazon. It helps us grow, and lets other readers discover our books.

As a thank you, we would love to send you a free digital copy of this book, and a **30%** discount code on your next cart value on our official websites:

www.orangeava.com

www.orangeava.in (For Indian Subcontinent)

☑ **Here's how:**

Leave a review for the book on Amazon.

Take a screenshot of your review, and send an email to **info@orangeava.com** (it can be just the confirmation screen).

Once, we receive your screenshot, we will send you the digital file, within 24 hours.

Thank you so much for your support – it means a lot to us!

Downloading the code bundles and colored images

Please follow the links or scan the QR codes to download the ***Code Bundles and Images*** of the book:

https://github.com/ava-orange-education/Ultimate-Modern-jQuery-for-Web-App-Development

The code bundles and images of the book are also hosted on ***https://rebrand.ly/mhy9h67***

In case there's an update to the code, it will be updated on the existing GitHub repository.

Errata

We take immense pride in our work at **Orange Education Pvt Ltd,** and follow best practices to ensure the accuracy of our content to provide an indulging reading experience to our subscribers. Our readers are our mirrors, and we use their inputs to reflect and improve upon human errors, if any, that may have occurred during the publishing processes involved. To let us maintain the quality and help us reach out to any readers who might be having difficulties due to any unforeseen errors, please write to us at :

errata@orangeava.com

Your support, suggestions, and feedback are highly appreciated.

DID YOU KNOW

Did you know that Orange Education Pvt Ltd offers eBook versions of every book published, with PDF and ePub files available? You can upgrade to the eBook version at **www.orangeava.com** and as a print book customer, you are entitled to a discount on the eBook copy. Get in touch with us at: **info@orangeava.com** for more details.

At **www.orangeava.com**, you can also read a collection of free technical articles, sign up for a range of free newsletters, and receive exclusive discounts and offers on AVA™ Books and eBooks.

PIRACY

If you come across any illegal copies of our works in any form on the internet, we would be grateful if you would provide us with the location address or website name. Please contact us at **info@orangeava.com** with a link to the material.

ARE YOU INTERESTED IN AUTHORING WITH US?

If there is a topic that you have expertise in, and you are interested in either writing or contributing to a book, please write to us at **business@orangeava.com**. We are on a journey to help developers and tech professionals to gain insights on the present technological advancements and innovations happening across the globe and build a community that believes Knowledge is best acquired by sharing and learning with others. Please reach out to us to learn what our audience demands and how you can be part of this educational reform. We also welcome ideas from tech experts and help them build learning and development content for their domains.

REVIEWS

Please leave a review. Once you have read and used this book, why not leave a review on the site that you purchased it from? Potential readers can then see and use your unbiased opinion to make purchase decisions. We at Orange Education would love to know what you think about our products, and our authors can learn from your feedback. Thank you!

For more information about Orange Education, please visit **www.orangeava.com**.

Table of Contents

1. **Getting Started with jQuery** **1**
    - Introduction 1
    - Structure 1
    - Brief Overview of jQuery 1
    - Getting Started using jQuery and How it Works 3
        - *Effortlessly Handle Events* 4
        - *Animation and Effects with Ease* 4
    - Compelling Reasons to Choose jQuery 5
    - Downloading and Adding jQuery to Your HTML 6
        - *Obtaining jQuery* 6
        - *Integrating jQuery into Your HTML* 6
        - *Verify jQuery Integration* 7
    - Using jQuery with CDN 8
    - Browser Dev Tools 12
    - Conclusion 14
2. **Selection of Page Elements and DOM Element Selection jQuery** **16**
    - Introduction 16
    - Structure 16
    - Selection of Page Elements and DOM Element Selection with jQuery 17
    - Basic Selectors 17
    - Attribute Selectors 19
    - Pseudo Selectors 20
    - DOM Traversal 21
    - Filtering Elements 23
    - Chaining Methods 26
    - Conclusion 28

3. Element Hide and Show Methods and Animation Effects **29**
Introduction 29
Structure 29
`Hide` and `Show` Methods 29
Exercise: Element hide and Show Methods and Animation effects 32
`fadeIn` and `fadeOut` Methods 34
Fading Effects with jQuery Elements 35
`slideUp` and `slideDown` Methods 37
Custom Animations with jQuery 40
CSS positioning properties 40
position 41
margin 41
transform 41
z-index 42
Creating Custom Animations with jQuery Exercise 43
Conclusion 46
Multiple Choice Questions 47
Answers 48
4. Manipulating Element Content and Inserting Elements **49**
Introduction 49
Structure 49
Manipulating element content with jQuery 49
Appending and prepending content 50
Clearing element content 51
Exercise: Adding new content and elements to the page 51
Inserting elements with jQuery 53
The Power of `.after()` and `.before()` 53
Wrapping elements 54
Inserting elements outside of the selected element 54
Advanced techniques 55
Exercise: Clone and update with replace page elements 55
Conclusion 56

Multiple Choice Questions 57
Answers 58
5. DOM Manipulation and Selection 59
Introduction 59
Structure 59
Adding and removing classes with jQuery 59
Understanding classes in HTML 60
Adding classes 60
Removing classes 60
Dynamically creating and modifying elements 61
Creating new elements 61
Modifying elements 62
Removing elements 62
Selecting and manipulating multiple elements 63
Parent elements 63
Child elements 63
Siblings 64
Advanced techniques 64
Cloning elements 64
Replace elements 66
Removing wrapping elements 66
Exercise: *Adding, removing, and toggling element classes* 67
Conclusion 69
Multiple Choice Questions 70
Answers 70
6. jQuery Dynamic List Project - Interactive Elements 71
Introduction 71
Structure 71
Creating a Dynamic List with jQuery 71
Interactive Elements with jQuery 72
Learning Outcomes 73
Exercise: Create an Interactive List with jQuery 74

Summary 76

Conclusion 77

Points to Remember 77

Multiple Choice Questions 79

Answers 79

7. CSS Properties and Element Attributes 80

Introduction 80

Structure 80

Getting and Setting CSS Properties with jQuery 80

Example: Changing Background Color on Button Click 81

Getting and Setting Element Attributes with jQuery 82

Retrieving and Modifying Element Dimensions with jQuery 83

Example: Toggle CSS Classes on Button Click 84

Exercise: Get the Style Properties of an Element 85

Exercise: Getting and Setting Element Attributes with jQuery 87

Exercise: Get the Dimensions of Page Elements with jQuery Methods 91

Conclusion 93

Multiple Choice Questions 93

Answers 94

8. Traversing Page Elements 95

Introduction 95

Structure 95

Traversing Descendants of Page Elements with jQuery 95

Exercise: Traversing Descendants of Page Elements with jQuery Selection 96

Traversing Ancestors of Page Elements with jQuery 99

Traversing Siblings of Page Elements with jQuery 100

Exercise: Traversing Siblings Page Elements and Other Selections with jQuery 101

Filtering Page Elements to Select them with jQuery 103

Selecting Elements Based on Visibility and State 104

Conclusion 108

Multiple Choice Questions 109
Answers 110
9. jQuery Data and Element Index Method 111
Introduction 111
Structure 112
Saving values into the element object with the jQuery data method 112
jQuery Data Method `.data()` 112
Saving Values with `.data()` 112
Retrieving Data 113
Removing Data 113
Exercise `data()` example 114
Index of Page Element Index Method `.index()` 116
Using `.index()` 116
Element Position 117
Exercise: Use the `get()` method to return the DOM element object 119
Exercise: Make a selection of page elements with jQuery and return the `index()` value of the selected element 121
Conclusion 124
Multiple Choice Questions 125
Answers 125
10. Handling Events with jQuery 126
Introduction 126
Structure 127
Understanding Event Handling 127
jQuery Event Methods 128
`.click()` 128
`.hover()` 129
`.submit()` 131
`.keypress()` 133
Mouse Events 134
`.hover()` 134

`.mouseup()` 135
`.mousedown()` 135
`.mouseout()` 135
`.mouseover()` 136
`.mouseleave()` 136
`.mouseenter()` 137
`.mousemove()` 137
jQuery mouse moves events listeners and hover events 137
jQuery to listen for keyboard events and get values from the event object 140
jQuery form Events on submit and more 143
Conclusion 146
11. Advanced Event Handling Techniques 147
Introduction 147
Structure 147
Event delegation 148
The `.on()` method 148
Exercise: Attach events with the on Method with more powerful events 148
Understanding Event Bubbling and Propagation 151
Exercise: jQuery scroll event on Browser Events and Window events 153
Conclusion 156
Multiple Choice Questions 157
Answers 158
12. jQuery AJAX Methods and Callback Options 159
Introduction 159
Structure 160
Introduction to AJAX with jQuery 160
Exercise: AJAX example connects to an external file and loads the contents directly into a page element 161
Exercise: jQuery AJAX method and callback options 163
Streamlined AJAX with Shorthand Methods 167

Callback Options for Handling AJAX Responses 168
Get JSON data with jQuery get method........ 170
GET shorthand Methods jQuery `getScript` and `getJSON` methods 173
Conclusion........ 175
Multiple Choice Questions........ 176
Answers 177
Conclusion 178
Multiple Choice Questions........ 179
Answers 181
Index........ 182

CHAPTER 1

Getting Started with jQuery

Introduction

Welcome to the introduction chapter of jQuery, the JavaScript library that redefines web development. In this first chapter, we embark on a journey into the world of jQuery, understanding its significance and why it's a vital tool in modern web development. We'll walk you through the process of downloading and seamlessly integrating jQuery into your projects, ensuring you're equipped with the essential resources. Additionally, we'll explore the concept of using jQuery through a Content Delivery Network (CDN) for faster loading and enhanced reliability. By the end of this chapter, you'll have a solid foundation for harnessing jQuery's power to create dynamic, interactive web applications that captivate users and streamline your development workflow. Let's begin our journey into the realm of jQuery.

Structure

In this chapter, we will discuss the following topics:

- Getting Started using jQuery and How it Works
- Downloading and Adding jQuery to your HTML
- Using jQuery with CDN

Brief Overview of jQuery

In the dynamic landscape of web development, creating interactive and engaging user experiences has become paramount. As websites and web applications evolve to meet the increasing demands of users, developers seek tools that streamline the process of adding interactivity and responsiveness to their projects. This is where jQuery steps in—a versatile and powerful JavaScript library that has revolutionized the way developers approach client-side scripting.

To fully appreciate the impact of jQuery, it's essential to understand the context in which it emerged. In the early days of web development, JavaScript was primarily used for simple tasks like form validation and basic interactivity. However, as web applications grew more complex and user expectations soared, developers were confronted with the challenges of cross-browser compatibility and convoluted DOM manipulation. These obstacles led to the birth of jQuery.

jQuery, introduced by John Resig in 2006, was a game-changer. It abstracted and standardized many of the intricacies of JavaScript, providing a concise and efficient way to interact with the Document Object Model (DOM)—the structure that represents a web page. With jQuery, developers could write less code and achieve more, as it offered a simplified syntax for common tasks such as element selection, event handling, and animations.

Traditional DOM manipulation required verbose code and careful consideration of cross-browser differences. jQuery addressed this challenge by offering a consistent API that abstracted away browser idiosyncrasies. Developers could now target and modify elements with ease, drastically reducing the time and effort required for such tasks.

One of the most significant pain points in web development was ensuring that a website worked seamlessly across various browsers. jQuery played a pivotal role in standardizing behavior, enabling developers to write code that behaved consistently across different browsers.

jQuery's plugin architecture paved the way for a vibrant ecosystem of plugins that extended its core functionality. From sliders and carousels to form validation and AJAX interactions, developers could tap into an expansive library of pre-built solutions to expedite their development process.

Creating animations and adding visual effects using raw JavaScript was a complex endeavor. jQuery's animation capabilities abstracted these complexities, allowing developers to create eye-catching animations and transitions with minimal effort.

Handling user interactions and events was a cornerstone of web development. jQuery introduced an intuitive event handling system that simplified attaching event listeners and responding to user actions, enhancing the interactivity of web applications.

As you embark on this journey to harness the power of jQuery, you'll discover a wealth of knowledge and techniques that enable you to build dynamic, interactive, and user-friendly web applications. This foundational chapter marks the beginning of your exploration into jQuery's capabilities and its transformative impact on modern web development.

jQuery makes it easy to get started with building interactive and dynamic web content. With basic knowledge of HTML and CSS, you can start creating engaging content. jQuery is just a JavaScript library and knowledge of JavaScript is helpful for the understanding and debugging of code.

jQuery provides an easy-to-use solution for web developers to add smooth animations, handle web page interactions and events, navigate page elements for selection, update and manipulate element properties and contents, and make AJAX requests for data.

It is designed for anyone who wants to learn jQuery, with prior HTML and CSS experience. Learn by example, each lesson has its own challenge to help you get more familiar with specific coding objectives. Source code is included that will help guide you through the lesson content with helpful tips and resources.

jQuery is used because of its ease of use, making it simple to create amazing animations and web page experiences. There is a large community for documentation and tutorials. It works across browsers and standardizes the experience so that all the browsers display the same way. There are a vast number of plugins, which can help create even more wonderful things with code. The code is also easier to read as the functions used in jQuery are simple and have semantic meaning.

Getting Started using jQuery and How it Works

In the ever-evolving landscape of web development, jQuery stands as a beacon of efficiency and innovation. It's not just a library; it's a game-changer that has redefined the way we build interactive web applications.

Understanding jQuery's Essence: At its core, jQuery is a fast, small, and feature-rich JavaScript library. Its primary objective is to simplify the process of DOM manipulation and event handling, making it easier for developers to create stunning user experiences. With a clear and concise syntax, jQuery abstracts the complexities of raw JavaScript, allowing developers to achieve remarkable results with fewer lines of code.

jQuery allows for the streamlining of web development. The significance of jQuery becomes evident when we consider the challenges that developers faced before its advent. The web development landscape was plagued by browser inconsistencies, convoluted DOM manipulation, and the arduous task of creating engaging animations and effects. jQuery addressed these pain points and more.

Consider the common task of selecting and manipulating HTML elements on a webpage. In raw JavaScript, this could be a cumbersome process involving different methods for different browsers. jQuery simplifies this process, providing a unified API for selecting, traversing, and modifying DOM elements.

```
// Raw JavaScript
const element = document.getElementById("myElement");
element.style.color = "red";

// jQuery equivalent
$("#myElement").css("color", "red");
```

Effortlessly Handle Events

Handling user interactions and events is fundamental to modern web applications. jQuery offers a consistent and intuitive way to attach event listeners and respond to user actions.

```
// Raw JavaScript
const button = document.getElementById("myButton");
button.addEventListener("click", function() {
    console.log("Button clicked!");
});

// jQuery equivalent
$("#myButton").click(function() {
    console.log("Button clicked!");
});
```

Animation and Effects with Ease

Creating animations and effects was once a complex endeavor. jQuery's animation methods simplify the process, enabling developers to create visually appealing transitions effortlessly.

```
// Raw JavaScript animation
const element = document.getElementById("animatedElement");
element.style.transition = "width 2s";
element.style.width = "300px";

// jQuery animation
$("#animatedElement").animate({ width: "300px" }, 2000);
```

Compelling Reasons to Choose jQuery

Here are some compelling reasons to choose jQuery:

- **Cross-Browser Compatibility**

One of the most frustrating challenges in web development is ensuring your code works consistently across different browsers. jQuery abstracts away browser differences, providing a consistent experience for users.

- **Rich Ecosystem of Plugins**

jQuery's plugin architecture has led to the creation of an extensive library of plugins, offering ready-made solutions for a wide range of functionalities, from form validation to complex UI components.

- **Enhanced Productivity**

By simplifying complex tasks and reducing the amount of code needed, jQuery significantly boosts developer productivity, allowing them to focus on the creative aspects of web development.

- **Learning Curve**

jQuery's intuitive syntax and well-documented API make it accessible even to developers who are new to JavaScript, accelerating their learning curve and enabling them to create impressive web applications faster.

- **Embrace jQuery's Power**

As you delve deeper into this book, you'll discover the intricate details of jQuery's methods, explore real-world use cases, and master the art of building captivating web applications. jQuery isn't just a library; it's a gateway to unlocking the potential of interactive web development. So, let's embark on this journey together and harness the full power of jQuery to craft remarkable user experiences on the web.

Downloading and Adding jQuery to Your HTML

Now that we understand the power of jQuery, it's time to equip ourselves with the tools we need to harness its potential. We'll walk you through the process of obtaining the jQuery library and seamlessly integrating it into your HTML files. There are many versions of jQuery, and it is recommended to use the latest 3.* version. jQuery is designed to simplify the HTML DOM tree traversal and manipulation of page elements. It provides an excellent way to create CSS animations and handle events and AJAX requests.

Obtaining jQuery

Before we can start using jQuery, we need to get our hands on the library itself. Thankfully, jQuery can be easily obtained from the official website, using multiple ways as follows:

- **Downloading Directly**: Visit the official jQuery website https://jquery.com/download/ and choose the version of jQuery you want to use. You can either download the compressed or uncompressed version of the library.

It is recommended to use the compressed version, as it saves bandwidth and is the smaller file size with whitespace removed. The uncompressed would only be used for debugging.

- **Content Delivery Network (CDN)**: Alternatively, you can include jQuery directly from a CDN. This has the advantage of potentially improving load times for your users if they've already visited other sites that use the same CDN.

CDN source: https://developers.google.com/speed/libraries#jquery

Integrating jQuery into Your HTML

Once you have downloaded the jQuery library, you need to integrate it into your HTML files. Here's a step-by-step guide:

1. **Create a New Folder**: Organize your project files and create a new folder named `js` within your project directory. This is where we'll store the jQuery file.

2. **Place jQuery File**: Move the downloaded jQuery file (for example, **`jquery-3.6.0.min.js`**) into the **`js`** folder you just created.
3. **Link to jQuery**: In your HTML file, typically just before the closing **`</body>`** tag, include the following code to link to the jQuery file:

    ```
    <script src="js/jquery-3.6.0.min.js"></script>
    ```

This code tells the browser to load the jQuery library from the specified location. Make sure to adjust the path if your project structure differs.

Verify jQuery Integration

To ensure that jQuery has been successfully integrated into your project, let's perform a simple test. Open your HTML file and add the following script just below the jQuery inclusion:

```
<script>
  // jQuery test
  $(document).ready(function() {
    alert("jQuery is working!");
  });
</script>
```

This code creates a simple jQuery script that triggers an alert when the document is ready. When you load your HTML file in a browser, you should see an alert box with the message **`jQuery is working!`**.

You can also use the browser editor and check to see if jQuery is loaded.

Use either **`$`** or **`jQuery`** in the browser console to check if jQuery is ready:

```
> $
<· f (e,t){return new S.fn.init(e,t)}
> jQuery
<· f (e,t){return new S.fn.init(e,t)}
```

Figure 1.1: *Using $ or jQuery to check if jQuery is ready*

Congratulations! You've successfully downloaded and integrated jQuery into your web project. With jQuery now seamlessly integrated into your development workflow, you're well on your way to creating dynamic, interactive, and visually engaging web applications. In the upcoming chapters, we'll explore jQuery's features in more depth and learn how to wield its capabilities to craft impressive user experiences. So, let's continue this journey and dive into the world of jQuery-powered web development!

Using jQuery with CDN

As we delve deeper into the world of jQuery, it's essential to explore alternative methods of accessing and utilizing this powerful library. In addition to downloading jQuery files locally, we can leverage the capabilities of CDNs to streamline the integration process and optimize the performance of our web applications. In this section, we'll delve into the concept of CDN and how to harness its advantages when incorporating jQuery into your web pages.

A CDN is a distributed network of servers strategically positioned around the world. The primary goal of a CDN is to deliver web content–such as images, scripts, stylesheets, and libraries–more efficiently to users by serving content from a server that is geographically closer to the user's location. This results in reduced latency, faster loading times, and improved reliability.

Incorporating jQuery via a CDN offers several benefits that enhance the performance and reliability of your web applications:

- CDNs distribute content across multiple servers, enabling browsers to fetch assets from the nearest server. This minimizes the distance data needs to travel, leading to faster loading times and improved user experiences.
- CDNs are optimized for caching, which means that when a user visits a site that uses a CDN-hosted jQuery version, their browser may have already cached the jQuery file from a previous visit to another site. This reduces redundant downloads and improves overall browser efficiency.
- CDNs are designed to handle high volumes of traffic and are often equipped with advanced security features, improving the overall reliability and availability of the resources they host.

To include jQuery in your project using a CDN, you don't need to download any files. Instead, you can reference the library directly from the CDN servers. Here's how you can do it:

```
<!–Include jQuery from Google CDN →

<script

s"c="https://ajax.googleapis.com/ajax/libs/jquery/3.6.0/jquery.min"js">
</script>
```

```
--- Include jQuery from Microsoft CDN -->
<script s"c="https://ajax.aspnetcdn.com/ajax/jQuery/jquery-3.6.0.min"js">
</script>
```

Choose one of the provided URLs (or explore other CDN options) and place the **<script>** tag in the **<head>** or just before the closing **</body>** tag of your HTML document.

By incorporating jQuery via a CDN, you tap into a global network of servers dedicated to optimizing the delivery of web content. This approach enhances your web applications' loading speed and overall performance, while also reducing the burden on your own hosting resources.

Following is the step-by-step guide on how to add jQuery to your HTML and create a simple element selection, event, and manipulation of element content with jQuery:

Exercise: Create a file add jQuery and write some jQuery Code:

1. Create an HTML file and add a page element.
2. Add the **script** tag link to the jQuery library.
3. Add a second **script** tag link to a new **js** file named **app1.js**.
4. Open the HTML in the browser and check if jQuery is on the page.
5. In **app1.js**, select the element using the same syntax as you would with CSS, for example, **$().**
6. Add a jQuery method named **.html()**.
7. Add a string value within **.html().**
8. Add the on('click') to the element and nest the update of the **html** inside.
9. Add a second **html()** chained to the on click method with another string value.

INDEX.HTML

```
<!DOCTYPE html>
        <html>
                <head><title>jQuery Course</title></head>
        <body>
                <div>Hello World</div>
```

```
            <script s”c=”
            https://ajax.googleapis.com/ajax/libs/jquery/3.6.0/jquery.m
            in”js”></script>
            <script s”c=”app1”js”></script>
    </body>
</html>
```

```
    APP1.JS ‘$(‘’iv’).‘n(‘cl’ck’,()=>{ ‘$(‘’iv’).ht‘l(‘Laurence Sve’is’);
}).ht‘l(‘Click’Me’);
```

Here are some simple examples of jQuery. We will provide more details about how they work in the upcoming chapters:

1. **Document Ready**

   Run code when the document is fully loaded and ready:

   ```
   $(document).ready(function() {
     // Your code here
   });
   ```

2. **Click Event**

   Execute code when an element is clicked:

   ```
   “$(“#myBut”on”).click(function() {
     // Your code here
   });
   ```

3. **Hide and Show**

   Toggle the visibility of an element:

   ```
     “$(“#toggleBut”on”).click(function() {
    “$(“#targetElem”nt”).toggle();
   });
   ```

4. **Adding CSS**

   Change CSS properties of an element:

   ```
   “$(“#myElem”nt”).c“s(“co”or“, “b”ue”);
   ```

5. **Adding Classes**

   Add a CSS class to an element:

   ```
   "$("#myElem"nt").addCla"s("highli"ht");
   ```

6. **Fading Effects**

   Apply fading effects to an element:

   ```
   "$("#fadeInBut"on").click(function() {
    "$("#fadingElem"nt").fadeIn();
   });
   "$("#fadeOutBut"on").click(function() {
    "$("#fadingElem"nt").fadeOut();
   });
   ```

7. **Slide Effects**

   Apply sliding effects to an element:

   ```
   "$("#slideDownBut"on").click(function() {
    "$("#slidingElem"nt").slideDown();
   });
   "$("#slideUpBut"on").click(function() {
    "$("#slidingElem"nt").slideUp();
   });
   ```

8. **AJAX Request**

   Fetch data from a server without reloading the page:

   ```
   $.ajax({
     ur": "data.j"on",
     success: function(data) {
       // Handle data
     },
     error: function() {
       // Handle error
     }
   });
   ```

9. **Mouse Hover**

   Perform actions when the mouse enters or leaves an element:

```
“$(“#hoverElem”nt”).hover(
  function() {
    // Mouse enter code
  },
  function() {
    // Mouse leave code
  }
);
```

10. **Animations**

    Create custom animations using jQu'ry's animate method:

```
“$(“#animateBut”on”).click(function() {
 “$(“#animatedElem”nt”).animate(
    {
      widt“: “20”px”,
      heigh“: “20”px”
    },
    1000 // Animation duration in milliseconds
  );
});
```

These examples provide a solid starting point for exploring jQuery's capabilities. Remember that jQuery offers a wide array of methods and functions for manipulating DOM elements, handling events, making AJAX requests, and creating dynamic animations. As you gain familiarity with these basics, you'll be well-prepared to dive deeper into more complex scenarios and build impressive web applications.

Browser Dev Tools

Using Chrome's Developer Tools (DevTools) is a powerful way to interact with and understand the inner workings of web pages. Here's a brief description of how to use it:

1. **Accessing DevTools**: Open Chrome and navigate to the web page you want to inspect. Right-click anywhere on the page and select "`Inspect`," or use the keyboard shortcut *Ctrl+Shift+I* (*Cmd+Opt+I* on Mac). This opens the DevTools panel.
2. **Elements Panel**: This panel allows you to view and modify the HTML and CSS of a page. You can inspect the DOM, change styles in real-time, and see how these changes affect the layout and appearance of the website.
3. **Console**: The Console tab is used for logging information as part of the JavaScript development process. You can also interact with the web page by executing JavaScript commands directly.
4. **Sources Panel**: This panel is where you can debug JavaScript by setting breakpoints, stepping through the code, and inspecting variables. You can view and edit source files directly in this panel.
5. **Network Panel**: It provides information about the network activity on the current page. You can see each file that is requested, its load time, and details like headers, response payloads, and HTTP status codes.
6. **Performance Panel**: Use this to analyze runtime performance of your web page. It helps in understanding the resources and time taken to render, script, and load the page.
7. **Application Panel**: This section is for inspecting all resources that are loaded, including IndexedDB or WebSQL databases, local and session storage, cookies, and cache.
8. **Audits Panel**: Now known as Lighthouse, this tool performs an analysis of the page and generates a report on performance, accessibility, progressive web apps, SEO, and more.
9. **Device Mode**: Simulate how your web pages look and behave on different devices and screen sizes.
10. **Customization and Settings**: Customize DevTools to fit your workflow. You can dock the panel in different parts of the screen, change themes, and even add extensions for additional functionality.

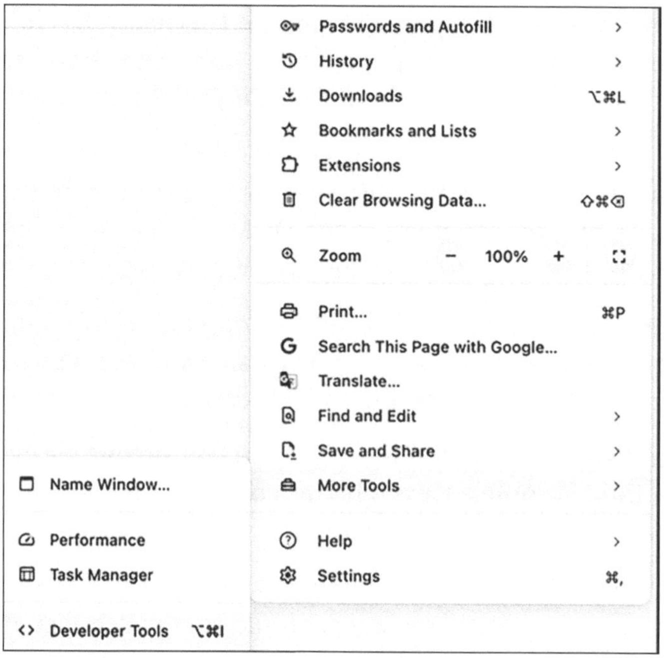

Figure 1.2: *DevTools*

These tools are incredibly helpful for web development, debugging, and learning more about web technologies. Remember, this is just an overview; each panel offers a deep set of features to explore.

Conclusion

As we conclude this introductory chapter, you've taken your first steps into the world of jQuery, a tool that is set to revolutionize your approach to web development. You've grasped the essence of jQuery and why it's indispensable in modern web development, as well as acquired practical skills for seamlessly integrating it into your projects. Whether you choose to download jQuery or leverage the efficiency of a Content Delivery Network (CDN), you're now equipped with the essential resources to harness jQuery's power. The journey has just begun, and the chapters ahead will delve deeper into jQuery's capabilities, enabling you to craft captivating, interactive web applications while simplifying your development workflow. So, fasten your seatbelt, for the jQuery adventure has just begun, and there's so much more to explore and create.

The upcoming chapter provides an in-depth exploration of using jQuery for web page manipulation, beginning with an understanding of the Document Object Model (DOM), a tree-like structure representing web page elements. Crucial for web content manipulation, the chapter explains jQuery's versatile selectors that target HTML elements by attributes, IDs, classes, or relationships, complete with syntax and examples. It then delves into manipulating these selected elements, detailing how to modify content, style, and attributes, and discusses adding or removing elements from the DOM. Additionally, it covers jQuery's DOM traversal methods for navigating the DOM tree to locate elements based on their relational context, essential for dynamic content manipulation. The chapter also introduces event handling with jQuery, illustrating how to interact with user actions like clicks and keyboard inputs, thereby enhancing web pages' interactivity. Furthermore, it highlights the power of chaining multiple jQuery methods for concise and readable code. Finally, it wraps up with best practices for using jQuery in DOM manipulation, emphasizing the importance of performance and maintainable code, making it a comprehensive guide for developers looking to enhance their web development skills with jQuery.

CHAPTER 2

Selection of Page Elements and DOM Element Selection jQuery

Introduction

Welcome to a crucial chapter where we delve into the essence of jQuery: the art of selecting page elements and traversing the Document Object Model (DOM). In this chapter, we will explore the fundamental tools at the heart of jQuery, starting with Basic Selectors that target elements by tags, classes, or IDs. We will then advance to Attribute Selectors and Pseudo Selectors, unveiling more intricate methods of pinpointing elements based on their attributes or states. Furthermore, we will navigate through the DOM with jQuery's traversal techniques, enhancing our ability to dynamically find and manipulate elements. Finally, we wrap up with Filtering Elements, providing a deeper understanding of refining selections for more complex and responsive web interfaces.

Structure

In this chapter, we will discuss the following topics:

- Basic Selectors
- Attribute Selectors
- Pseudo Selectors

- Traversing DOM Elements with jQuery
- Filtering Elements with jQuery

Selection of Page Elements and DOM Element Selection with jQuery

In the world of web development, the ability to select and manipulate DOM elements is paramount. jQuery equips developers with powerful tools to effortlessly navigate and manipulate the Document Object Model (DOM), allowing for dynamic and engaging web experiences. In this chapter, we will delve deep into the art of selecting DOM elements using jQuery.

Basic Selectors

Selecting elements on a web page is at the core of jQuery's capabilities. Basic selectors enable you to target elements by their HTML tags, classes, and IDs. Here's a glimpse of how it's done:

```
// Select by tag
$("p") // Selects all <p> elements

// Select by class
$(".highlight") // Selects elements with class "highlight"

// Select by ID
$("#header") // Selects the element with ID "header"
```

Exercise: Making selections of page elements:

1. Create an HTML file to interact with, including elements with IDs and classes.
2. Make a selection of the element using the tag, class, and ID. Output the jQuery element object into the console.
3. Create variables and assign the jQuery element objects and output them to the page.

HTML:

```
<!DOCTYPE html>
<html>
<head><title>jQuery Course</title></head>
<body>
<div>Hello World 1</div>
<div class="div2">Hello World 2</div>
<div id="div3">Hello World 3</div>
<script
src="https://ajax.googleapis.com/ajax/libs/jquery/3.6.0/jquery.m in.
js"></script>
<script src="app2.js"></script>
</body>
</html>
```

APP2.JS

```
console.log($('div'));
$('div').html('Hello');
console.log($('.div2'));
console.log($('#div3'));
console.log($('#div3, .div2'));
const $ele1 = $('div');
console.log($ele1);
$ele1.html('Hello 2');
const $ele2 = $('.div2');
console.log($ele2);
const $ele3 = $('#div3');
console.log($ele3);
const $ele4 = $('#div3, .div2');
console.log($ele4);
```

Attribute Selectors

Attribute selectors empower you to target elements based on their attributes and values. This is particularly useful for handling input validation and customization:

```
// Select by attribute
$("input[type='text']") // Selects all text input elements

// Select with specific attribute
$("[data-toggle]") // Selects elements with "data-toggle" attribute
```

Exercise: Select using the attribute:

HTML:

```
<!DOCTYPE html>
<html lang="en">
<head>
  <meta charset="UTF-8">
  <meta name="viewport" content="width=device-width, initial-scale=1.0">
  <title>Attribute Selector Example</title>
  <script src="https://code.jquery.com/jquery-3.6.0.min.js"></script>
</head>
<body>
  <h1>Attribute Selector Example</h1>
  <button data-toggle="modal">Open Modal</button>
  <button data-toggle="sidebar">Open Sidebar</button>
  <script src="script.js"></script>
</body>
</html>
```

JavaScript (script.js):

```
$(document).ready(function() {
  // Attach a click event to elements with data-toggle attribute
  $("[data-toggle]").click(function() {
```

```
    const target = $(this).data("toggle");
    alert(`Toggle ${target}`);
  });
});
```

In this example, we have two buttons, each with a data-toggle attribute set to different values. When a button is clicked, the script uses the attribute selector **`$("[data-toggle]")`** to target all elements with the data-toggle attribute. The click event handler then alerts a message indicating which element was toggled.

To run the exercise, create the HTML and JavaScript files in the same directory, and open the HTML file in a web browser. When you click the **`Open Modal`** or **`Open Sidebar`** button, you'll see an alert message indicating which element was toggled. This exercise demonstrates how to use the attribute selector to target elements based on their data attributes.

Pseudo Selectors

Pseudo selectors offer dynamic selection based on element states, such as **`:hover`**, **`:first-child`**, and **`:nth-child`**:

```
// Select the first <li> element inside <ul>
$("ul li:first-child")

// Select odd-numbered <tr> elements in a table
$("table tr:nth-child(odd)")
```

Exercise: Using jQuery, select the first list item and change its background color to blue:

HTML:

```
<!DOCTYPE html>
<html lang="en">
<head>
  <meta charset="UTF-8">
  <meta name="viewport" content="width=device-width, initial-scale=1.0">
  <title>Change CSS with jQuery</title>
    <script src="https://code.jquery.com/jquery-3.6.0.min.js"></script>
</head>
```

```
<body>
  <h1>Change CSS with jQuery</h1>
  <ul>
    <li>Item 1</li>
    <li>Item 2</li>
    <li>Item 3</li>
  </ul>
  <script src="script.js"></script>
</body>
</html>
```

JavaScript (script.js):

```
$(document).ready(function() {
    // Change CSS for the first list item
    $("ul li:first-child").css("color", "blue");
  });
```

In this example, we have an unordered list with three list items. The jQuery code in the **`script.js`** file uses the selector **`$("ul li:first-child")`** to target the first list item. It then uses the **`.css()`** method to change the text color of the first list item to blue.

To run the example, create the HTML and JavaScript files in the same directory, and open the HTML file in a web browser. You'll see a list with three items, and the text color of the first item will be changed to blue. This example demonstrates how to use jQuery to change the CSS properties of specific elements in a list.

DOM Traversal

jQuery simplifies the process of navigating the DOM hierarchy, allowing you to traverse through parent, children, and sibling elements with ease:

```
// Select the parent of an element
$("#childElement").parent()

// Select all direct children of an element
$("ul").children()
```

```
// Select the next sibling of an element
$(".current").next()
```

Here are the steps for Traversing Ancestors of Page Elements using parent methods with jQuery:

Exercise: Traverse to the ancestors of the selected element moving up towards the parent HTML element.

1. Select the button element, and when clicked, output the length of the **`parent()`** and **`parents()`**.
2. Select the elements that are ancestors of the element using **`parentsUntil()`** and select an element to stop at.
3. Use the **`each()`** to loop through the array of elements. Add a class to all the elements that are ancestors of the second button and have a class of main.

HTML:

```
<!DOCTYPE html>
<html>
<head><title>jQuery Course</title>
<style>
.box{
width:200px;
border:5px solid #ddd;
padding:20px;
margin:10px;
}
</style>
</head>
<body><nav class="main">
<div class="main">
<div xclass="div1">Hello World 1</div>
<div class="div2"><span>Hello World 2</span></div> <div class="div3"
id="div3">Hello World 3</div> <div class="div4">Laurence Svekis</div>
<input >
```

```
<div class="main">
<button id="btn1">1</button>
<button id="btn2">2</button>
</div>
<button id="btn1">3</button>
</div></nav>
<button id="btn1">4</button>
<script
src="https://ajax.googleapis.com/ajax/libs/jquery/3.6.0/jquery.m in.
js"></script>
<script src="app14.js"></script>
</body>
</html>
```

app14.js

```
$('#btn1').click(function(){
console.log($(this).parent().length);
console.log($(this).parents().length);
console.log($(this).parents());
console.log($(this).parents('.main'));
console.log($(this).parentsUntil('nav'));
})
$('#btn2').click(function(){
$(this).parents('.main').each(function(){
$(this).addClass('parentM');
})
})
```

Filtering Elements

Refine your selections by filtering elements that meet specific conditions. This enhances precision in manipulating specific parts of your webpage:

```
// Filter by even-numbered elements
$("li").filter(":even")
```

```
// Filter by elements containing specific text
$("p").filter(":contains('jQuery')")
```

Exercise: Using filtering to make a selection of specific elements and traverse to the result:

1. Add click events to all five-page buttons.
2. On clicking the first button, select an element collection and then traverse to the **`first()`**, **`last()`**, and **`eq()`** for selecting a specific element using the position in the collection, and apply styling to the resulting elements.
3. On clicking the second button, use **`filter()`** to select matching element results and apply styling to the resulting elements.
4. On clicking the third button, select the elements from the collection that do not match the request and apply styling to the resulting elements.
5. For the fourth and fifth buttons, try out variations of **`filter()`** and **`not()`** to make element selections traversing from the selected element, and apply styling to the matching results.

HTML:

```
<!DOCTYPE html>
<html>
<head>
<title>jQuery Course</title>
<style>
.box {
border: 1px solid #ddd;
padding: 5px;
color: red;
}
.box1 {
border: 1px solid #ddd;
padding: 5px;
color: blue;
}
```

```
.box2 {
border: 1px solid #ddd;
padding: 5px;
color: green;
}
</style>
</head>
<body>
<nav>
<div class="main">
<div class="div1">Hello World 1</div>
<div class="div2"><span>Hello World 2</span></div> <div class="div3"
id="div3">Hello World 3</div> <div class="div4">Laurence Svekis</div>
<input>
<button id="btn1">1</button>
<button id="btn2">2</button>
<button id="btn3">3</button>
<span>Hello</span>
</div>
</nav>
<button id="btn4">4</button>
<button id="btn5">5</button>
<script
src="https://ajax.googleapis.com/ajax/libs/jquery/3.6.0/jquery.m in.
js"></script>
<script src="app16.js"></script>
</body>
</html>
```

app16.js

```
$('#btn1').click(()=>{
console.log($('.main').children());
$main = $('.main').children();
$main.first().css('color','red');
```

```
$main.last().css('color','blue');
$main.eq(7).css('color','green');
$main.eq(6).css('background-color','green');
})
$('#btn2').click(()=>{
$main = $('.main').children();
$btns = $main.filter('button');
$main.filter('button').css('background-color','black'); $btns.css('color','
white');
})
$('#btn3').click(()=>{
$main = $('.main').children();
$btns = $main.not('button');
$main.not('button').css('background-color','purple'); $btns.css('color','
white');
})
$('#btn4').click(()=>{
$('.main div').not('.div1').css('color','red'); })
$('#btn5').click(()=>{
$('.main div').filter('div').css('color','green'); })
```

Chaining Methods

One of jQuery's strengths lies in its method chaining, enabling you to combine multiple methods into a single, concise line of code:

```
// Chain methods to select and manipulate an element
$("#myElement").addClass("highlight").slideUp(1000);
```

Exercise: How to chain multiple methods together:

HTML:

```
<!DOCTYPE html>
<html lang="en">
<head>
  <meta charset="UTF-8">
```

```
  <meta name="viewport" content="width=device-width, initial-scale=1.0">
  <title>Chaining Methods with jQuery</title>
  <script src="https://code.jquery.com/jquery-3.6.0.min.js"></script>
</head>
<body>
  <h1>Chaining Methods with jQuery</h1>
  <div id="box"></div>
  <button id="animateButton">Animate</button>
  <script src="script.js"></script>
</body>
</html>
```

JavaScript (script.js):

```
$(document).ready(function() {
  // Attach click event to the animate button
  $("#animateButton").click(function() {
    // Chain methods to animate the box
    $("#box")
      .css("background-color", "blue")
      .animate({ width: "200px" }, 1000)
      .delay(500)
      .fadeOut()
      .fadeIn()
      .slideUp();
  });
});
```

In this example, we have a box and a button. When the button with the ID **`animateButton`** is clicked, the jQuery code in the **`script.js`** file chains several methods together to create an animation sequence on the box:

1. The box's background color changes to blue.
2. The box's width gradually increases to 200px over 1 second.
3. The animation pauses for 500 milliseconds.

4. The box fades out and then fades back in.
5. The box slides up and disappears.

To run the example, create the HTML and JavaScript files in the same directory, and open the HTML file in a web browser. Click the **`Animate`** button to see the box animation sequence. This example demonstrates how to chain multiple jQuery methods to create a sequence of actions on an element.

By mastering the art of selecting DOM elements with jQuery, you're equipped to transform static web pages into dynamic, engaging experiences. Whether you're creating animations, handling user interactions, or fetching data, understanding element selection is crucial. The ability to select and manipulate elements is the cornerstone of effective jQuery usage.

Conclusion

This chapter has provided a thorough exploration of jQuery's capabilities in web development, emphasizing its power in DOM manipulation. We delved into how jQuery selectors enable precise targeting of HTML elements, essential for dynamic web content manipulation. The chapter also detailed practical approaches to altering element content, styles, and attributes, along with adding or removing elements. We examined jQuery's DOM traversal methods, crucial for navigating complex web structures, and introduced event handling for enhanced user interaction. Additionally, we highlighted the efficiency of chaining methods for concise and readable code. Finally, we underscored the importance of best practices in jQuery for optimized performance and maintainable code. This knowledge equips developers with the tools necessary for creating interactive, efficient, and user-friendly web applications.

In the next chapter, we will uncover a variety of tools to breathe life into your web pages. We will explore the **`'Hide'`** and **`'Show'`** methods, which allow you to toggle the visibility of elements, providing seamless transitions and interactive features. We will also delve into **`'Fade In'`** and **`'Fade Out'`** methods, enabling graceful opacity transitions. Additionally, we will cover '**`Slide Up`**' and '**`Slide Down`**' methods to add dynamic vertical motion to your web elements. Lastly, we will dive into the realm of custom animations, empowering you to create unique, eye-catching transitions tailored to your specific design needs.

CHAPTER 3

Element Hide and Show Methods and Animation Effects

Introduction

In the realm of web development, the ability to control the visibility and add animation effects to page elements can transform a static website into an interactive and engaging experience. jQuery offers a robust set of methods to achieve this, opening up a world of possibilities for creating dynamic web content. In this chapter, we will explore these methods, from simple hide and show techniques to more advanced fading and sliding effects, equipping you with the skills to breathe life into your web pages.

Structure

In this chapter, we will discuss the following topics:

- **`Hide`** and **`show`** methods
- **`Fade in`** and **`fade out`** methods
- **`slideUp`** and **`slideDown`** methods
- Custom animations with jQuery

Hide and Show Methods

jQuery provides the **`.hide()`** and **`.show()`** methods, which are used to control the visibility of HTML elements on a web page. These methods are commonly employed in web development to create interactive and dynamic user interfaces.

`.hide()`: Concealing Elements

The **`.hide()`** method does precisely what its name suggests – it conceals elements from view by setting their CSS display property to **none**. Here is how you can use it:

```
$("#elementToHide").hide();
```

The **`.hide()`** method is used to hide one or more selected elements by modifying their CSS properties, particularly the display property. When you hide an element using **`.hide()`**, it becomes invisible and no longer takes up space in the layout. Here is how it works:

```
$(selector).hide(speed, callback);
```

`selector`: This is a jQuery selector that specifies the element(s) you want to hide. It can be an element type, class, ID, or any other valid selector.

`speed` (optional): This parameter specifies the speed of the hiding animation. It can be one of the following values:

`slow`: Slow animation (600 milliseconds)

`fast`: Fast animation (200 milliseconds)

A numeric value: The duration of the animation in milliseconds

`callback` (optional): This is a function that gets executed after the **`.hide()`** operation is complete.

Example:

```
// Hide a specific element with ID "myElement" slowly
$("#myElement").hide("slow");


// Hide all <div> elements with class "hidden" quickly
$("div.hidden").hide("fast");
```

`.show()`: Revealing Hidden Elements

Conversely, the **`.show()`** method reveals hidden elements by changing their display property back to its default value, which is usually *block* or *inline*. Its usage is straightforward:

```
$("#elementToShow").show();
```

The `.show()` method is used to display one or more selected elements that have previously been hidden using `.hide()` or were initially hidden by default. It reverses the effect of the `.hide()` method, making the element(s) visible again. Here is how it works:

```
$(selector).show(speed, callback);
```

`selector`: This is a jQuery selector that specifies the element(s) you want to display.

`speed` (optional): This parameter specifies the speed of the showing animation, just like in **`.hide()`**.

`callback` (optional): This is a function that gets executed after the **`.show()`** operation is complete.

Example:

```
// Show a specific element with ID "myElement" slowly
$("#myElement").show("slow");

// Show all <div> elements with class "visible" quickly
$("div.visible").show("fast");
```

- **Toggle Visibility**: **`.hide()`** and **`.show()`** are often used together to toggle the visibility of elements. For example, you can hide a form when a **`Hide`** button is clicked and then show it again when a **`Show`** button is clicked.
- **Creating Animations**: These methods can be used to create simple animations, such as fading elements in and out or sliding them up and down.
- **Building Accordion Menus**: In combination with event handlers, these methods are used to create accordion menus where clicking one section hides others and reveals the clicked section.
- **Showing and Hiding Tooltips and Popovers**: Tooltips and popovers in web applications are often implemented using these methods to control their display.

In summary, the **`.hide()`** and **`.show()`** methods in jQuery are fundamental for controlling the visibility of elements on a web page. They are versatile tools that can be used in various scenarios to create interactive and dynamic user interfaces.

Exercise: Element hide and Show Methods and Animation effects

Click elements, hide the clicked elements. Add a button that will show the elements.

1. Select all the **`div's`** from the page
2. Select the first one using **`first()`** and the last one using **`last()`**
3. Add a click event to the **`div's.`** When clicked, it should select the element from the click event that was clicked. Be careful, as this will select the nested elements. Update the html to say clicked. Update the element with text or ready. Then apply the **`hide()`** function to the element
4. Add an event to the button which shows all the **`div's`**, and the H1

Example of hide and show being used in code:

HTML for this section :

```
<!DOCTYPE html>
<html>
<head><title>jQuery Course</title>
</head>
<body>
<div>Hello World 1</div>
<div class="div2">Hello World 2</div>
<div id="div3">Hello World 3</div>
<button>Show</button>
<script
src="jquery.m in.js"></script>
<script src="app3.js"></script>
</body>
</html>
```

JavaScript JS code :

```
console.log($('div').first());
const val = '<h1>Laurence Svekis</h1>';
```

```
$('div').first().html(val);
$('div').last().text(val);
$('div').click((e)=>{
const $el = $(e.target);
console.log($el);
$el.html('clicked');
$(e.target).text('Ready');
$(e.target).hide("slow");
});
$('button').click((e)=>{
$('div').show("fast");
$('h1').show(4000);
});
function eleClicker(e){
console.log(e);
}
```

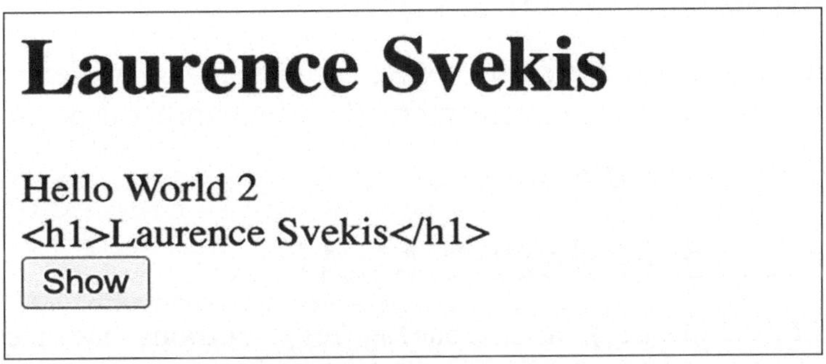

***Figure 3.1**: Example output from Exercise*

Here is a breakdown of the JavaScript code:

- `console.log($('div').first());`: This line selects the first `<div>` element on the page using jQuery and logs it to the console.
- `const val = '<h1>Laurence Svekis</h1>';`: This line creates an HTML string containing an `<h1>` element with the text **Laurence Svekis**.
- `$('div').first().html(val);`: This line selects the first `<div>` element and sets its HTML content to the value stored in the `val` variable (that is, it replaces the content of the first `<div>` with the `<h1>` element).

- **`$('div').last().text(val);`**: This line selects the last **`<div>`** element and sets its text content to the value stored in the **`val`** variable (that is, it changes the text of the last **`<div>`** to **Laurence Svekis**).
- **`$('div').click((e) => { ... });`**: This code attaches a click event handler to all **`<div>`** elements. When a **`<div>`** is clicked, the handler function is executed. It changes the HTML content of the clicked **`<div>`** to **clicked**, changes the text content to **Ready**, and then hides the **`<div>`** element with a **slow** animation.
- **`$('button').click((e) => { ... });`**: This code attaches a click event handler to the button element. When the button is clicked, it shows all the **`<div>`** elements with a **fast** animation and also shows the **<h1>** element with a duration of 4000 milliseconds (4 seconds).
- **function `eleClicker(e) { ... }`**: This appears to be a defined function **`eleClicker`** that takes an event object **`e`** as a parameter, but it is not used or invoked in the provided code.

In summary, the JavaScript code uses jQuery to manipulate the HTML elements on the page, changing their content and behavior in response to user interactions. The code demonstrates basic DOM manipulation and event handling with jQuery.

`.toggle()`: Switching Between Hide and Show

The **`.toggle()`** method allows you to toggle the visibility of an element with each click, providing a simple way to create interactive elements like expandable sections:

```
$("#toggleElement").toggle();
```

`fadeIn` and `fadeOut` Methods

The **`.fadeIn()`**, **`.fadeOut()`**, and **`.fadeToggle()`** methods are used to create smooth, gradual transitions between visible and hidden states.

`.fadeIn()`: Gradual Appearance

The **`.fadeIn()`** method smoothly transitions an element from invisible to fully visible. You can specify the animation duration:

```
$("#fadeInElement").fadeIn(1000); // 1000 milliseconds (1 second)
```

`.fadeOut()`: Gradual Disappearance

Conversely, the **`.fadeOut()`** method gradually fades an element out of view. Like **`.fadeIn()`**, you can set the animation duration:

```
$("#fadeOutElement").fadeOut(1000);
```

`.fadeToggle()` : Toggling Fade In/Out

The **`.fadeToggle()`** method toggles between fading in and fading out. It's ideal for creating toggleable elements:

```
$("#fadeToggleElement").fadeToggle(1000);
```

Fading Effects with jQuery Elements

Now, we will learn fading effects with jQuery:

1. Make all the page `divs` clickable
2. Create variables to track the number of times the elements were clicked, and the number of elements that are currently hidden.
3. Update the text or html of the element after its clicked
4. Add a click event to the button, once clicked shows, toggles and applies different fading effects to the elements.
5. Create a variable that will toggle the opacity of the button element, every time it's clicked it should change the opacity from 0.5 to 1 and back.

HTML Code

```
<div>Hello World 1</div>
<div class="div2">Hello World 2</div>
<div id="div3">Hello World 3</div>
<button>Show</button>
```

Source Code JS

```
$('div').first().html(val);
let counter = 0;
let hiddenEle = 0;
let fader = 0.5;
$('div').click(function(e){
//$(e.target).fadeOut(1000);
console.log($(this));
console.log($(this).text());
$(this).fadeOut(1000,()=>{
```

```
counter++;
hiddenEle++;
const temp = `<h3>Counter ${counter}</h3>`; $(this).html(temp);
$('button').text(`Show (${hiddenEle})`); });
})
$('button').click((e)=>{
//$('div').fadeIn("slow");
/*
$('div').fadeToggle('slow',function(){ $(this).text('Was toggled');
})
*/
$('div').toggle(1500);
hiddenEle = 0;
$('button').text(`All Showing`);
$('button').fadeTo('slow',fader,()=>{
if(fader == 0.5){
fader = 1;
}else{
fader = 0.5;
}
})
})
```

JavaScript Section:

`const val = '<h3>Laurence Svekis</h3>';`: Initializes a constant variable **`val`** with an HTML string containing an **`<h3>`** element.

`let counter = 0;`: Declares a variable counter and initializes it to 0. It's used to keep track of the number of clicks.

`let hiddenEle = 0;`: Declares a variable **`hiddenEle`** and initializes it to 0. It tracks the number of hidden elements.

`let fader = 0.5;`: Declares a variable fader and initializes it to 0.5. It's used to control the opacity when fading elements.

`$('div').first().html(val);` : Selects the first `<div>` element and sets its HTML content to the value stored in the `val` variable (that is, it replaces the content of the first `<div>` with the `<h3>` element).

`$('div').click(function(e){ ... })`: Attaches a click event handler to all `<div>` elements. When a `<div>` is clicked:

- It fades out over 1 second (1000 milliseconds).
- Logs the clicked `<div>` to the console.
- Logs the text content of the clicked `<div>` to the console.
- Fades in a new `<h3>` element with text `Counter {counter}` and updates the counter.
- Updates the button text to `Show` (`{hiddenEle}`) to show the number of hidden elements.

`$('button').click((e)=>{ ... })`: Attaches a click event handler to the button.

- Toggles the visibility of all `<div>` elements over 1.5 seconds (1500 milliseconds).
- Resets `hiddenEle` to 0 and updates the button text to `All Showing`.
- Fades the button's opacity with a `callback` function that toggles fader between 0.5 and 1.

In summary, this code demonstrates how to use jQuery to manipulate HTML elements, handle click events, and create fading effects on elements. It also keeps track of the number of hidden elements and updates the button text accordingly.

`slideUp` and `slideDown` Methods

The `.slideUp()`, `.slideDown()`, and `.slideToggle()` methods to add sliding effects to page elements:

`.slideUp()`: Conceal with Slide

The `.slideUp()` method hides elements by sliding them up. You can control the animation duration:

```
$("#slideUpElement").slideUp(1000);
```

`.slideDown()`: Reveal with Slide

On the flip side, `.slideDown()` reveals elements by sliding them down. Animation duration is customizable:

```
$("#slideDownElement").slideDown(1000);
```

`.slideToggle()`: Toggle Sliding

The `.slideToggle()` method toggles between sliding an element up and down. It's perfect for creating collapsible sections:

```
$("#slideToggleElement").slideToggle(1000);
```

Exercise: Slide effect with jQuery

1. Hide the `show` button
2. Add a click event on the hide button which will hide all the page `divs` using the `slideUp()` and invoke a function that will toggle both buttons
3. The second show button should now be visible, add a click event on the button to show all the `divs` using the `slideDown()` function.
4. Add a click event to each `div` that does `slideToggle()` which should hide the `div` when clicked.

HTML Code

```
<div>Hello World 1</div>
<div class="div2">Hello World 2</div>
<div id="div3">Hello World 3</div>
<button id="btn1">Hide</button>
<button id="btn2">Show</button>
```

```
JavaScript Code
$('#btn2').hide();

$('#btn1').click(() => {
  $('div').slideUp('slow', doneFun);
});

$('#btn2').click(() => {
  $('div').slideDown('fast', doneFun);
```

```
});

$('div').click(function() {
  $(this).slideToggle();
});

function doneFun() {
  console.log('slide done');
  $('#btn1').toggle();
  $('#btn2').toggle();
}
```

`$('#btn2').hide();`

This line initially hides the element with the ID **btn2**. This means that the button with ID **btn2** will not be visible when the page loads.

`$('#btn1').click(() => { ... });`

This code attaches a click event handler to the element with ID **btn1**. When the **btn1** button is clicked, the following action occurs:

`$('div').slideUp('slow', doneFun);`

All **<div>** elements on the page slide up slowly (over 600 milliseconds) using the **slideUp** method. After the sliding animation is complete, the **doneFun** function is called.

`$('#btn2').click(() => { ... });`

This code attaches a click event handler to the element with ID **btn2**. When the **btn2** button is clicked, the following action occurs:

`$('div').slideDown('fast', doneFun);`

All **<div>** elements on the page slide down quickly (over 200 milliseconds) using the slideDown method. After the sliding animation is complete, the **doneFun** function is called.

`$('div').click(function() { ... });`

This code attaches a click event handler to all **<div>** elements on the page. When any **<div>** is clicked, the following action occurs:

`$(this).slideToggle();`: The clicked **`<div>`** element toggles its sliding state. If it's currently hidden, it will slide down, and if it's currently visible, it will slide up.

```
function doneFun() { ... }
```

This is a custom JavaScript function named **`doneFun`**. It is called when the slide animation (**`slideUp`** or **`slideDown`**) on the **`<div>`** elements is completed. This function does the following:

Logs **`slide done`** to the console.

Toggles the visibility of the **`btn1`** and **`btn2`** buttons using **`.toggle()`**. This means that if **`btn1`** is currently visible, it will be hidden, and if **`btn2`** is hidden, it will be made visible.

In summary, this code creates a simple interactive webpage with two buttons (**`btn1`** and **`btn2`**) and multiple **`<div>`** elements. Clicking **`btn1`** will slide up the **`<div>`** elements, and clicking **`btn2`** will slide them down. Additionally, clicking any **`<div>`** element toggles its visibility. The **`doneFun`** function logs messages and toggles the buttons to provide feedback to the user.

Custom Animations with jQuery

Beyond the standard methods, jQuery enables you to craft custom animations using the **`.animate()`** method. This method grants you precise control over CSS properties and animation duration:

```
$("#customAnimationElement").animate(
  {
    width: "200px",
    opacity: 0.5
  },
  1000
);
```

CSS positioning properties

To use the **`.animate()`** method in jQuery effectively, you often need to understand and manipulate the CSS positioning properties. CSS positioning properties determine how an element is positioned within its containing element or the document. In jQuery animations, you can animate changes to these properties to create various visual effects.

Here are the key CSS positioning properties that you might need to use with the **.animate()** method, along with examples:

position

The **position** property specifies the positioning method used for an element.

Common values include relative, absolute, fixed, and static.

Example:

```
.box {
  position: relative;
}
top, right, bottom, left:
```

These properties are often used with elements whose position is set to relative, absolute, or fixed.

They specify the offset from the element's normal position.

Example:

```
.box {
  position: relative;
  top: 20px;
  left: 30px;
}
```

margin

The **margin** property controls the space outside an element's border.

You can animate the margin to change an element's position smoothly.

Example:

```
.box {
  margin-left: 10px;
}
```

transform

The **transform** property allows you to apply transformations like translation, rotation, and scaling to an element.

It's often used with animations to create complex effects.

Example:

```
.box {
  transform: translate(50px, 20px);
}
```

z-index

The `z-index` property controls the stacking order of elements with the same position value.

It's useful when you want to animate elements in and out of view, changing their stacking order.

Example:

```
.box1 {
  z-index: 1;
}

.box2 {
  z-index: 2;
}
```

Here's an example of how you might use these properties with jQuery's `.animate()` method:

```
$(document).ready(function() {
  $("#moveButton").click(function() {
    $(".box").animate(
      {
        left: "+=50px",
        top: "+=30px",
        margin: "10px",
        transform: "rotate(45deg)",
        zIndex: 2,
      },
      1000 // Duration in milliseconds
```

```
    );
  });
});
```

In this example, clicking the **moveButton** will animate **the .box** elements. It changes their left and top positions, margin, transform (rotation), and z-index. This showcases how jQuery's **.animate()** method can smoothly transition these CSS properties to create dynamic visual effects.

Creating Custom Animations with jQuery Exercise

Select and move page elements and apply custom animation effects to selected elements.

1. Add position relative or absolute to the page elements you want to move
2. Select all the elements, with button 1 click apply various animations with styling values
3. With button 2 click add different custom animations to the page elements

HTML Code

```
<div class="div1">Hello World 1</div>
<div class="div2">Hello World 2</div>
<div class="div3" id="div3">Hello World 3</div>
<button id="btn1">1</button>
<button id="btn2">2</button>
```

CSS Code

```
div{
left:100px;
position:relative;
border:1px solid #ddd;
width:120px;
}
```

JavaScript code

```
$('#btn1').click(() => {
  $('.div1').text(`I'm moving`);
  $('.div1').animate({
    left: "+=20",
    opacity: 0.5
  }, 1000, () => {
    $('.div1').text(`STOPPED`);
  });
  $('.div2').animate({
    left: "+=50",
    fontSize: "20px"
  }, 3000, () => {
    $('.div2').text(`Laurence Svekis`);
  });
  $('.div3').animate({
    top: "+=50",
    width: "150px",
    height: "150px"
  }, 1000, () => {
    $('.div2').text(`Laurence Svekis`);
  });
})

$('#btn2').click(() => {
  $('.div1').text(`I'm moving`).animate({
    left: "-=50",
    opacity: 1
  }, 1000, () => {
    $('.div1').text(`STOPPED`);
  });
  $('.div3').animate({
    top: "-=50",
```

```
    width: "50px",
    height: "35px"
  }, 1000, () => {
    $('.div2').text(`DONE`);
  });
})
```

Button 1 (`#btn1`) Click Event:

When **`btn1`** is clicked, the following animations occur:

- **`$('.div1').text(I'm moving);`**: This line changes the text content of all elements with the class **`div1`** to **`I'm moving`**.
- **`$('.div1').animate({ ... }, 1000, () => { ... });`**: This animates all elements with the class "div1" with the following properties:
- **`left: "+=20"`**: The elements move 20 pixels to the right.
- **`opacity: 0.5`**: The opacity of the elements becomes 0.5 (semi-transparent).
- The animation lasts for 1000 milliseconds (1 second).
- After the animation is complete, a callback function is executed, changing the text content of **`div1`** elements to **`STOPPED`**.
- **`$('.div2').animate({ ... }, 3000, () => { ... });`**: This animates all elements with the class **`div2`** with the following properties:
- **`left: "+=50"`**: The elements move 50 pixels to the right.
- **`fontSize: "20px"`**: The font size of the elements becomes 20 pixels.
- The animation lasts for 3000 milliseconds (3 seconds).
- After the animation is complete, a callback function is executed, changing the text content of **`div2`** elements to **`Laurence Svekis`**.
- **`$('.div3').animate({ ... }, 1000, () => { ... });`**: This animates all elements with the class **`div3`** with the following properties:
- **`top: "+=50"`**: The elements move 50 pixels down.
- **`width: "150px"`**: The width of the elements becomes 150 pixels.
- **`height: "150px"`**: The height of the elements becomes 150 pixels.
- The animation lasts for 1000 milliseconds (1 second).
- After the animation is complete, a callback function is executed, changing the text content of **`div2`** elements to **`Laurence Svekis`**.

Button 2 (`#btn2`) Click Event:

When `btn2` is clicked, the following animations occur:

- `$('.div1').text(I'm moving).animate({ ... }, 1000, () => { ... });`: This line first changes the text content of all elements with the class "div1" to "I'm moving" and then animates them with the following properties:
- `left: "-=50"`: The elements move 50 pixels to the left.
- `opacity: 1`: The opacity of the elements becomes 1 (fully visible).
- The animation lasts for 1000 milliseconds (1 second).
- After the animation is complete, a `callback` function is executed, changing the text content of `div1` elements to `STOPPED`.
- `$('.div3').animate({ ... }, 1000, () => { ... });`: This animates all elements with the class `div3` with the following properties:
- `top: "-=50"`: The elements move 50 pixels up.
- `width: "50px"`: The width of the elements becomes 50 pixels.
- `height: "35px"`: The height of the elements becomes 35 pixels.
- The animation lasts for 1000 milliseconds (1 second).
- After the animation is complete, a callback function is executed, changing the text content of `div2` elements to `DONE`.

In summary, this code uses jQuery to create animations on elements with different classes based on button clicks. It changes text content, moves elements, changes opacity, font size, width, and height of elements, and provides feedback to the user using callback functions when animations are complete.

Conclusion

We have covered jQuery's arsenal for controlling element visibility and adding animation effects to your web pages. Armed with these techniques, you will have the power to captivate your audience with engaging user interfaces, responsive animations, and interactive content. In the next chapter, we will learn about manipulating the contents of web page elements and inserting new elements using the power of jQuery.

Multiple Choice Questions

1. What is the jQuery method used to hide an element?
   a) `.hideElement()`
   b) `.visibility('hidden')`
   c) `.hide()`
   d) `.disappear()`
2. Which jQuery method is used to display a hidden element?
   a) `.reveal()`
   b) `.show()`
   c) `.display()`
   d) `.visible()`
3. How can you animate an element to fade out using jQuery?
   a) `.fadeOut()`
   b) `.animateFadeOut()`
   c) `.hide('fade')`
   d) `.fade()`
4. Which method should you use to hide an element with a sliding animation in jQuery?
   a) `.slideOut()`
   b) `.slideUp()`
   c) `.slideHide()`
   d) `.hideSlide()`

5. In jQuery, how can you animate an element to change its height over 400 milliseconds?
    a) `$('element').animate({height: 'toggle'}, 400);`
    b) `$('element').changeHeight('400ms');`
    c) `$('element').heightAnimate(400);`
    d) `$('element').resizeHeight({duration: 400});`

Answers

1. c)`.hide()`
2. b)`.show()`
3. a)`.fadeOut()`
4. b)`.slideUp()`
5. a) `$('element').animate({height: 'toggle'}, 400);`

Chapter 4
Manipulating Element Content and Inserting Elements

Introduction

In this chapter, we will dive into the exciting world of manipulating the contents of web page elements and inserting new elements using the power of jQuery. Whether you're a seasoned web developer or just getting started, mastering these techniques will significantly enhance your ability to create dynamic and interactive web pages.

Structure

In this chapter, we will cover the following topics:

- Manipulating element content with jQuery
- Inserting elements with jQuery
- Inserting elements outside of the selected element

Manipulating element content with jQuery

Understanding element content

Before we embark on the journey of content manipulation, let's first understand how web page elements store their content. In HTML, elements can contain both text and HTML content. Text content is the visible part of an element, such as the text within a paragraph or heading. HTML content, on the other hand, includes child elements, making up the hierarchical structure of a web page.

Changing text content

One of the most common tasks when working with web page elements is changing their text content. jQuery provides the `.text()` method, which allows you to set or retrieve the text content of an element. You can use this method to:

- **Update the text of a heading**

  ```
  $("h1").text("New Heading Text");
  ```

- **Retrieve the current text of an element**

  ```
  let currentText = $("p").text();
  ```

Modifying HTML content

In addition to changing text content, you often need to manipulate the HTML content of elements. jQuery's `.html()` method comes in handy for this purpose. This method enables you to:

- **Replace the HTML content of a div:**

  ```
  $("div").html("<p>New HTML content</p>");
  ```

- **Append HTML content to an element:**

  ```
  $("ul").append("<li>New List Item</li>");
  ```

- **Remove elements by setting their HTML content to an empty string:**

  ```
  $("#removeMe").html("");
  ```

Appending and prepending content

Dynamic content updates are essential for creating interactive web pages. jQuery offers the `.append()` and `.prepend()` methods to add content to the end or beginning of selected elements, respectively. You can:

- **Append a new paragraph to a div:**

  ```
  $("div").append("<p>Appended paragraph</p>");
  ```

- **Prepend a heading to a section:**

  ```
  $("section").prepend("<h2>Prepended heading</h2>");
  ```

Clearing element content

There are situations where you need to remove all content from an element. The `.empty()` method in jQuery allows you to do just that:

- **Remove all content from a list:**

  ```
  $("ul").empty();
  ```

- **Clear the contents of a div:**

  ```
  $("#clearMe").empty();
  ```

Understanding these methods for manipulating element contents in jQuery is essential for creating dynamic and responsive web pages. Whether you're updating text, modifying HTML, or managing content within elements, jQuery's tools make these tasks efficient and accessible, enhancing the interactivity of your web applications.

Exercise: Adding new content and elements to the page

In this exercise, we will explore various ways to add new content and elements to a web page using jQuery. We'll also interact with user input and perform operations like appending, prepending, and removing elements.

Step 1: Creating new page elements

Create a loop to generate clickable buttons, each displaying a different text content. These buttons will later be used to interact with the page.

```
let counter = 0;


for (let i = 0; i < 10; i++) {
  counter++;
  const $span = $(`<span>Hello :${counter}</span>`);
  $span.text('New');
  $('.div2').append($span);
}
```

In this step, we create 10 clickable buttons and append them to the element with the class `.div2`.

Step 2: Handling button clicks

Attach click event handlers to the buttons generated in step 1. When a button is clicked, its text content will be logged to the console.

```
for (let i = 0; i < 3; i++) {
  const $btn = $(`<button>After ${i + 1}</button>`);
  $('.div4').after($btn);

  $btn.click(function () {
    console.log($(this).text());
  });

  $(`<button>Before ${i + 1}</button>`).insertBefore('.div4').click(-
function () {
    console.log($(this).text());
  });
}
```

Here, we attach event handlers to buttons, both after and before the element with the class .div4. When a button is clicked, it logs its text content to the console. This demonstrates the use of **`.after()`**, **`.insertBefore()`**, and event handling.

Step 3: More element manipulation

On click of the first button with the id btn1, get the text value of the input element and perform several operations:

1. Set the text content of .div1 to the input value.
2. Append the input value to **`.div2`**.
3. Prepend the input value to **`.div3`**.
4. Remove the element with the class **`.div4`**.

```
$('#btn1').click(() => {
  const val = $('input').val();
  $('.div1').text(val);
  $('.div2').append(val);
  $('.div3').prepend(val);
```

```
  $('.div4').remove();
});
```

Step 4: Dynamic element creation

On click of the second button with the id **btn2**, create a new div element with an incremental counter and perform the following:

1. Append the new div element to **.div3**.
2. Append the new div element to **.div3** again using **.appendTo()**.
3. Log the created div element to the console.

```
$('#btn2').click(() => {
  counter++;
  const $div = $(`<div>Hello :${counter}</div>`);
  $('.div3').append($(`<div>Hello :${counter}</div>`));
  $(`<div>Hello :${counter}</div>`).appendTo('.div3');
  console.log($div);
});
```

In this step, we create new div elements, append them to **.div3**, and log one of the created elements to the console, showcasing the use of **.append()** and **.appendTo()**.

These exercises demonstrate various techniques for adding new content and elements to a web page, both inside and outside of selected elements. It also illustrates how to interact with user input and manipulate the page dynamically using jQuery.

Inserting elements with jQuery

In this section, we'll explore powerful techniques for inserting elements into a web page using jQuery. These methods provide you with fine-grained control over where and how new elements are added, making your web pages more dynamic and interactive.

The Power of `.after()` and `.before()`

The **.after()** and **.before()** methods in jQuery are essential tools for inserting new elements before or after an existing element. These methods open up a world of possibilities for dynamic content insertion. Here's how they work:

- **.after()**: This method allows you to insert content or elements immediately after the selected element. It's great for adding elements like buttons, messages, or additional content after an existing element.

```
$('.existing-element').after('<div>New Content After</div>');
```

- **.before()**: Similar to **.after()**, **.before()** inserts content or elements immediately before the selected element. It's useful for adding content before an element, such as a prepended message or an icon.

```
$('.existing-element').before('<div>New Content Before</div>');
```

Wrapping elements

Mastering the art of wrapping elements using jQuery's **.wrap()** and **.unwrap()** methods is crucial for creating structured layouts and styling flexibility. Here's how these methods work:

- **.wrap()**: This method adds a wrapping element around each selected element. It's particularly useful for encapsulating elements in containers, allowing you to apply CSS styles or manipulate grouped elements as a unit.

```
$('.selected-elements').wrap('<div class="wrapper"></div>');
```

- **.unwrap()**: Conversely, **.unwrap()** removes the parent wrapper element from the selected elements, leaving the wrapped content intact. It's handy when you want to remove unnecessary containers.

```
$('.selected-elements').unwrap();
```

Inserting elements outside of the selected element

Sometimes, you may need to insert elements outside of the initially selected element. jQuery provides **.insertBefore()** and **.insertAfter()** methods for this purpose:

- **.insertBefore()**: Use this method to insert an element or content before the selected element. It's valuable for moving or duplicating content to a different location in the DOM.

```
$('<div>New Content</div>').insertBefore('.existing-element');
```

- **.insertAfter()**: Similar to **.insertBefore()**, **.insertAfter()** inserts content or elements after the selected element, allowing you to reposition content dynamically.

```
$('<div>New Content</div>').insertAfter('.existing-element');
```

Advanced techniques

In addition to the fundamental techniques discussed earlier, there are advanced scenarios to explore:

- **Cloning elements**: jQuery's **`.clone()`** method allows you to create copies of existing elements, which can then be inserted into different parts of the page.

  ```
  const $copy = $('.original-element').clone();
  $copy.insertAfter('.target-element');
  ```

- **Inserting elements based on user interactions**: You can combine event handlers, user interactions, and insertion methods to dynamically add elements based on user actions, enhancing the interactivity of your web page.

These advanced techniques provide you with the tools needed to create dynamic, responsive, and interactive web pages using jQuery. Whether you're adding elements before or after, wrapping elements for styling, or exploring more complex scenarios, jQuery empowers you to take full control of your web development projects.

Exercise: Clone and update with replace page elements

In this exercise, we will explore two different actions to manipulate page elements using jQuery: replacing selected elements with new content and cloning an element to add it to an existing element.

Step 1: Replacing page elements with new content

When the first button (**`#btn1`**) is clicked, we will replace selected elements with new content using both the **`.replaceAll()`** and **`.replaceWith()`** methods.

```
$('#btn1').click(() => {
  // Using .replaceAll() to replace selected elements with new content
  $('<h3>Hello</h3>').replaceAll('.div3');

  // Using .replaceWith() to replace the entire .div2 with new content
  $('.div2').replaceWith('<h3>Hello 3</h3>');
});
```

In this step, when **#btn1** is clicked:

a. The **.replaceAll('.div3')** method replaces all elements with the class **.div3** with a new **<h3>** element containing "**Hello**."

b. The **.replaceWith('<h3>Hello 3</h3>')** method replaces the entire **.div2** element with a new **<h3>** element containing "**Hello 3**."

Step 2: Cloning and adding elements

When the second button (**#btn2**) is clicked, we will clone the input element with the id **myIn** and add the cloned element to an existing element using the **.clone()** and **.prependTo()** methods.

```
$('#btn2').click(() => {
  // Clone the input element with id 'myIn'
  const $ele = $('#myIn').clone();

  // Log the cloned element to the console
  console.log($ele);

  // Clone and prepend the last input element to the first div element
  $('input').last().clone().prependTo('div');
});
```

In this step, when **#btn2** is clicked:

a. We use **const $ele = $('#myIn').clone();** to clone the input element with the id **myIn** and store it in the variable **$ele**.

b. We log the cloned element to the console using **console.log($ele);**.

c. We clone the last input element (**$('input').last()**) and prepend it to the first <div> element within the page using **.clone().prependTo('div')**.

These actions demonstrate how you can replace selected elements with new content and clone elements to add them to existing elements, enhancing the dynamic nature of your web page.

Conclusion

We introduced the **.html()** and **.text()** methods, which are crucial for manipulating the inner HTML and text content of elements. These methods not only allow for the retrieval of current content but also enable the updating of this content with new data.

We discussed methods like **`.append()`**, **`.prepend()`**, **`.after()`**, and **`.before()`**, each serving a unique purpose in terms of where new content is inserted relative to selected elements. This section is particularly insightful for developers looking to create dynamic, content-rich web pages. It underscores jQuery's role in simplifying the process of DOM manipulation, making it more accessible and less error-prone compared to traditional JavaScript coding.

Coming up next, "DOM *Manipulation and Selection*" is a pivotal chapter for web developers seeking to master jQuery, a powerful JavaScript library known for simplifying client-side scripting. This chapter provides an in-depth exploration of jQuery's capabilities in selecting and manipulating the Document Object Model (DOM) of a web page. It starts by introducing the basic yet powerful jQuery selectors, which allow developers to easily locate and target elements within the HTML document using simple syntax. Following this, the chapter dives into various methods of DOM manipulation, demonstrating how jQuery can be used to alter element properties, styles, and content dynamically and interactively. This chapter is crucial for understanding how jQuery streamlines the process of interacting with web page elements, making it an invaluable resource for creating responsive and interactive web applications.

Multiple Choice Questions

1. What jQuery method is used to get or set the HTML content of an element?

   a) `.html()`

   b) `.content()`

   c) `.innerHTML()`

   d) `.getText()`

2. Which method is used to get or set the text content of an element in jQuery?

   a) `.text()`

   b) `.textContent()`

   c) `.innerText()`

   d) `.getString()`

3. How do you insert content to the end of each element in the set of matched elements in jQuery?

   a) `.appendTo()`

   b) `.prependTo()`

   c) `.after()`

   d) `.append()`

4. Which jQuery method is used to insert content at the beginning of each element in the set of matched elements?

   a) `.prepend()`

   b) `.before()`

   c) `.insertBefore()`

   d) `.startWith()`

5. What jQuery method would you use to remove all child nodes of the set of matched elements from the DOM?

   a) `.delete()`

   b) `.remove()`

   c) `.empty()`

   d) `.clear()`

Answers

1. a) `.html()`

2. a) `.text()`

3. d) `.append()`

4. a) `.prepend()`

5. c) `.empty()`

CHAPTER 5

DOM Manipulation and Selection

Introduction

In this chapter, we'll take a deeper dive into the world of Document Object Model (DOM) manipulation and selection using jQuery. Building upon the foundational concepts covered earlier, we'll explore advanced techniques to modify the structure of a web page dynamically. By the end of this chapter, you'll have a thorough understanding of how to wield jQuery's power to manipulate the DOM effectively.

Structure

In this chapter, we will cover the following topics:

- Adding and removing classes with jQuery
- Dynamically creating and modifying elements
- Selecting and manipulating multiple elements

Adding and removing classes with jQuery

In this section, we'll explore the fundamental concepts of working with classes in HTML and how jQuery empowers us to dynamically add and remove classes from elements.

Understanding classes in HTML

HTML uses the class attribute to apply CSS styles and group elements with similar characteristics. Classes act as hooks, allowing you to target and style elements easily. Here are key points to understand:

Class attribute: In HTML, elements can have one or more classes assigned to them using the class attribute. Multiple classes are separated by spaces. For example:

```
<div class="box red">This is a red box.</div>
```

Styling with CSS: CSS rules target elements by their class names, enabling consistent styling across multiple elements. For instance, the following CSS rule styles all elements with the class box:

```
.box {
  border: 2px solid black;
  padding: 10px;
}
```

Adding classes

jQuery simplifies the process of adding one or more classes to selected elements using the **`.addClass()`** method. This method is invaluable for applying CSS styles dynamically or for identifying elements for JavaScript interactions.

Syntax:

```
$(element).addClass(class1 [, class2, class3, ...]);
Example:
// Add the class 'highlight' to a button when clicked
$('button').click(function () {
  $(this).addClass('highlight');
});
```

Removing classes

To remove specific classes from elements, jQuery provides the **`.removeClass()`** method. This is useful when classes are no longer needed or when you want to alter the appearance or behavior of elements.

Syntax:

```
$(element).removeClass(class1 [, class2, class3, ...]);
```

Example:

```
// Remove the class 'active' from a navigation item when it's no longer
active
$('.nav-item').removeClass('active');
```

By understanding the role of classes in HTML and mastering jQuery's **`.addClass()`** and **`.removeClass()`** methods, you gain the ability to dynamically style elements, create interactive user interfaces, and respond to user interactions effectively. These techniques are fundamental to building dynamic and responsive web applications.

Dynamically creating and modifying elements

In this section, we'll delve into the power of jQuery when it comes to dynamically creating and modifying elements within the Document Object Model (DOM) of a web page. These techniques allow you to enhance user interfaces, add content on the fly, and create truly dynamic web experiences.

Creating new elements

Dynamically creating HTML elements is a core capability of jQuery. You can generate entirely new elements, specify their attributes and content, and then insert them into the DOM at the desired location. Here's how it works:

- Creating a new element: You can create a new HTML element by specifying its tag name within the jQuery function. For example:

  ```
  const newDiv = $('<div></div>');
  ```

- Setting attributes: To set attributes for the new element, you can chain the **`.attr()`** method. For instance:

  ```
  const newLink = $('<a></a>').attr('href', 'https://example.com');
  ```

- Adding content: You can also add content to the new element by using the .html() or **`.text()`** methods:

  ```
  const newParagraph = $('<p></p>').text('This is a new paragraph.');
  ```

- Inserting into the DOM: To place the newly created element into the DOM, you can use methods like **.append()**, **.prepend()**, **.before()**, or **.after()** on existing elements. For example:

```
newDiv.appendTo('.container'); // Appends newDiv to an element
with class 'container'
```

Modifying elements

Once you have elements in the DOM, jQuery provides methods to modify them, such as adding content or moving elements around within the page structure. Key methods include:

- **.append()**: This method adds content or elements to the end of the selected element. It's commonly used for inserting elements like paragraphs, images, or lists.

```
$('.container').append('<p>New content at the end.</p>');
```

- **.prepend()**: Similar to **.append()**, **.prepend()** adds content or elements to the beginning of the selected element.

```
$('.container').prepend('<p>New content at the beginning.</p>');
```

- **.before()** and **.after()**: These methods insert content or elements before or after the selected element.

```
$('.element').before('<div>Before</div>');
$('.element').after('<div>After</div>');
```

Removing elements

jQuery provides methods to remove elements and their contents from the DOM. Understanding when and how to use these methods is essential:

- **.remove()**: This method removes the selected element and all of its descendants from the DOM.

```
$('.element-to-remove').remove();
```

- **.empty()**: The .empty() method removes all child elements and content from the selected element, leaving the element itself intact.

```
$('.element-to-empty').empty();
```

Mastering these techniques for creating, modifying, and removing elements allows you to create dynamic and interactive web pages, respond to user actions, and dynamically update content as needed. These skills are central to building responsive and engaging web applications.

Selecting and manipulating multiple elements

In this section, we'll delve into the world of selecting and manipulating multiple elements using jQuery. These techniques enable precise control over elements within the DOM, allowing you to navigate hierarchical structures, target specific children, and work with related siblings.

Parent elements

Using jQuery's `.parent()` method, you can easily select and manipulate the parent elements of a given element. This is particularly useful for hierarchical navigation and styling. Here's how it works:

- **Selecting the parent**: The `.parent()` method selects the immediate parent element of the matched elements. For example:

  ```
  $('.child-element').parent(); // Selects the parent element(s) of elements with class 'child-element'
  ```

- **Styling the parent**: You can apply CSS styles or manipulate the parent elements to change their appearance or behavior. This is handy for creating hover effects or adjusting the layout based on the parent element.

Child elements

The `.children()` method in jQuery allows you to select and manipulate child elements of a parent element. This provides precise control over specific elements within a container. Here's how it works:

- **Selecting children**: `.children()` selects all direct child elements of the matched elements. For example:

  ```
  $('.parent-element').children(); // Selects all direct child elements of elements with class 'parent-element'
  ```

- **Manipulating children**: You can apply changes, add content, or perform operations on the selected child elements. This is helpful for dynamic form validation, creating interactive menus, or modifying specific sections of a page.

Siblings

The `.siblings()` method is a powerful tool for selecting and manipulating elements that share the same parent. This is particularly useful for handling related elements in dynamic interfaces. Here's how it works:

- Selecting siblings: .siblings() selects all sibling elements of the matched elements, excluding the matched elements themselves. For example:

  ```
  $('.selected-element').siblings(); // Selects all siblings of el-
  ements with class 'selected-element'
  ```

- Working with siblings: You can apply changes to sibling elements, hide or show related content, or trigger actions on elements that share the same parent. This is crucial for building tabbed interfaces, image galleries, or multi-step forms.

Understanding how to select and manipulate parent elements, child elements, and siblings with jQuery provides you with precise control over your web page's structure and behavior. These techniques are essential for building complex and interactive user interfaces, where elements often interact and affect one another based on user actions.

Advanced techniques

In this section, we'll explore advanced techniques for DOM manipulation using jQuery. These techniques allow you to perform more sophisticated operations, such as cloning elements, replacing elements, and optimizing your document's structure by removing unnecessary wrapping elements.

Cloning elements

The `.clone()` method in jQuery allows you to create copies of existing elements in the DOM. Cloning is essential for various scenarios, including replicating elements in dynamic forms, creating image galleries, or duplicating content. Here's how it works:

- **Cloning an element**: You can clone an element by calling the `.clone()` method on a jQuery object representing the element you want to duplicate. For example:

  ```
  const $originalElement = $('.original-element');
  const $cloneElement = $originalElement.clone();
  ```

- **Modifying cloned elements**: Once you have cloned an element, you can modify its attributes, content, or other properties as needed. Cloning provides a starting point for customizing elements.
- **Inserting cloned elements**: You can insert the cloned element into the DOM, either at the same location or elsewhere, using methods like `.append()`, `.prepend()`, `.insertBefore()`, or `.insertAfter()`.

Exercise: Cloning an Element and Modifying Its Content

1. Start by selecting the element with the class original-element.
2. Clone this element using the **`clone()`** method and store the cloned element in a variable **`$cloneElement`**.
3. Modify the text content of the cloned element to "**`I am a clone!`**" using the **`text()`** method.
4. Finally, append the modified clone to the element with the ID cloned-elements-container.

HTML

```
<div class="original-element">Hello, World!</div>
<div id="cloned-elements-container"></div>
```

jQuery

```
$(document).ready(function() {
    const $originalElement = $('.original-element');
    const $cloneElement = $originalElement.clone();

    // Modify the content of the cloned element
    $cloneElement.text("I am a clone!");

    // Append the cloned element to a specific container
    $('#cloned-elements-container').append($cloneElement);
});
```

Cloning is a powerful technique for creating dynamic interfaces, managing user-generated content, and maintaining consistency across your web application.

Replace elements

The `.replaceWith()` method in jQuery allows you to swap one element for another, altering the DOM structure dynamically. This is useful when you want to update content or replace an element with a different one without affecting its surrounding elements. Here's how it works:

1. **Replacing an element**: To replace an element, you call the `.replaceWith()` method on the jQuery object representing the element you want to replace. For example:

   ```
   const $existingElement = $('.existing-element');
   const $newElement = $('<div>New Content</div>');
   $existingElement.replaceWith($newElement);
   ```

   The code selects an existing element with the class existing-element, creates a new div element with the text "`New Content`", and then replaces the existing element in the DOM with this new div element. The original existing element is removed from the DOM as a result of this operation.

2. **Inserting new element**: The original element is removed from the DOM and replaced by the new element you specify. This operation maintains the document's integrity while allowing you to update content dynamically.

3. **Updating content**: You can replace elements with new content, whether it's HTML, text, or other elements. This is commonly used for dynamic content loading and updating portions of a page without requiring a full page refresh.

Removing wrapping elements

The `.unwrap()` method in jQuery allows you to remove unnecessary wrapping elements from around a selected element, optimizing your document's structure. This is useful when you want to simplify the DOM or eliminate extraneous container elements. Here's how it works:

1. **Removing wrapping elements**: To remove wrapping elements, you call the `.unwrap()` method on the jQuery object representing the element you want to unwrap. For example:

   ```
   $('.unwanted-wrapper').unwrap();
   ```

2. **Optimizing structure**: This method simplifies the DOM structure by removing unnecessary container elements. It's commonly used in

scenarios where elements are initially wrapped for styling or layout purposes but need to be unwrapped for easier manipulation.

3. **Retaining content**: The content of the unwrapped element remains intact; only the wrapper is removed. This ensures that the content and layout of your page are not affected.

These advanced techniques empower you to perform complex DOM manipulations with ease. Whether you're creating dynamic forms and galleries, or optimizing your document structure, understanding how to clone elements, replace elements, and remove unnecessary wrapping elements is invaluable for building rich and responsive web applications.

Exercise: Adding, removing, and toggling element classes

In this exercise, you'll work with jQuery to add, remove, and toggle classes on HTML elements. These actions will help you understand how to manipulate element classes dynamically in response to user interactions.

Step 1: Click event and `hasClass()`

We begin by adding a click event to all the `<div>` elements on the page.

HTML

```
<div class="blue">Click me (I'm blue)</div>
<div>Click me (No color)</div>
<div class="red">Click me (I'm red)</div>
<div>Click me (No color)</div>
<div class="blue">Click me (I'm blue)</div>
```

CSS

```
    .red {
        color: red;
    }
    .blue {
        color: blue;
    }
```

jQuery

```
$('div').click(function(){
  console.log($(this)); // Output the clicked element
  const boo = $(this).hasClass('red'); // Check if the element has the 
'red' class
  console.log(boo); // Output the result (true or false)
  if(boo){
    $(this).text('Already Red!!!'); // If it has the 'red' class, set 
text
  } else {
    $(this).text('Changed to Red'); // If not, set different text
  }
  $(this).addClass('red'); // Add the 'red' class
  $(this).removeClass('blue'); // Remove the 'blue' class
})
```

In this step:

1. We add a click event to all **<div>** elements on the page, and when clicked, proceed as follows.
2. Check if the clicked element has the class **'red'** using **.hasClass()**.
3. Based on the result, we change the text of the element.
4. We then add the **'red'** class to the clicked element and remove the **'blue'** class.

Step 2: Adding the 'blue' class

We add an event to the first button (**#btn1**) that adds the **'blue'** class to all **<div>** elements.

```
$('#btn1').click(() => {
  $('div').addClass('blue'); // Add the 'blue' class to all div elements
});
```

In this step:

When the first button is clicked (**#btn1**), we use **.addClass()** to add the **'blue'** class to all **<div>** elements. This changes their background color to blue.

Step 3: Toggling classes with the second button

We add an event to the second button (**#btn2**) that toggles both the **'red'** and **'blue'** classes on all **<div>** elements.

```
$('#btn2').click(() => {
  $('div').toggleClass('red'); // Toggle the 'red' class
  $('div').toggleClass('blue'); // Toggle the 'blue' class
});
```

In this step:

1. When the second button is clicked (**#btn2**), we use **.toggleClass()** to toggle both the **'red'** and **'blue'** classes on all **<div>** elements. This allows you to switch between different styles dynamically.
2. By completing this exercise, you'll gain a practical understanding of how to add, remove, and toggle classes on elements using jQuery. These skills are valuable for creating interactive and responsive user interfaces.

Conclusion

This chapter has provided readers with an in-depth exploration of DOM manipulation and selection using jQuery, building upon the foundational concepts introduced earlier. Throughout this chapter, readers have gained a comprehensive toolkit of jQuery methods for altering the structure of web pages, including the addition, removal, and relocation of elements. We've uncovered techniques for precise element selection, such as targeting parent, child, and sibling elements with the **.parent()**, **.children()**, and **.siblings()** methods. Additionally, we've delved into more advanced practices, including the creation of element duplicates using **.clone()**, the removal of child elements with **.empty()**, the replacement of elements via **.replaceWith()**, and the removal of wrapping elements using **.unwrap()**. Moreover, we've explored the dynamic management of classes and the dynamic creation and modification of elements.

In the upcoming chapter, we'll dive into creating interactive elements with jQuery through a practical project: the jQuery Dynamic List Project. You'll apply your jQuery skills to build a dynamic list that lets users add and remove items. We'll guide you through using jQuery methods to modify the list's content and structure and adding event listeners for full interactivity. Additionally, you'll learn how to style the list and interactive elements with CSS. This hands-on project is the perfect opportunity to put your jQuery knowledge to work and gain real-world experience in creating engaging web elements. Get ready to make your web projects come alive with interactivity and style!

Multiple Choice Questions

1. Which jQuery method allows you to remove all child elements from a selected element?
   a. `.empty()`
   b. `.remove()`
   c. `.detach()`
   d. `.unwrap()`
2. Which method in jQuery is used to create copies of existing elements?
   a. `.append()`
   b. `.clone()`
   c. `.replaceWith()`
   d. `.unwrap()`
3. Which jQuery method is used to remove a wrapping element from around a selected element?
   a. `.unwrap()`
   b. `.remove()`
   c. `.empty()`
   d. `.detach()`

Answers

1. a) `.empty()`
2. b) `.clone()`
3. c) `.unwrap()`

CHAPTER 6

jQuery Dynamic List Project - Interactive Elements

Introduction

In this chapter, we'll embark on a practical project using jQuery, where we'll create a dynamic list with interactive elements. This project will allow readers to apply their knowledge of jQuery to build a real-world, interactive feature that can be used in web applications. Let's dive in!

Structure

In this chapter, we will discuss the following topics:

- Creating a Dynamic List with jQuery
- Interactive Elements with jQuery

Creating a Dynamic List with jQuery

In this section, we will create a dynamic list with jQuery:

1. **Project Overview**: We'll begin by understanding the project's scope. We aim to create a dynamic list that users can interact with, allowing them to add and remove items as needed. This list will dynamically update its content and structure based on user actions.

2. **HTML Structure**: We'll define the HTML structure for our list, including an input field for adding new items, a button to submit new items, and an area to display the list of items.
3. **CSS Styling**: We'll use CSS to style our list and make it visually appealing. This will include styling the list items, buttons, and the overall layout.
4. **jQuery for Interactivity**: We'll leverage jQuery to add interactivity to our list. Readers will learn how to use jQuery methods to:
    a. **Add Items**: We'll use `.append()` or `.prepend()` to add new items to the list when the user submits them.
    b. **Remove Items**: We'll implement a mechanism to remove items from the list when the user clicks a delete button associated with each item. This will involve using event delegation to handle dynamic elements.

Event Delegation

Event delegation in jQuery is a technique used to handle events efficiently, especially when dealing with multiple elements that can trigger the same event. It's particularly useful in scenarios where elements are dynamically added to the DOM (that is, not present when the page initially loads) or when you want to minimize the number of event handlers you attach to elements.

In traditional event handling, you attach an event handler directly to each target element. However, this approach can lead to performance issues if there are many elements because each element gets its own event handler. Also, if new elements are added dynamically to the DOM, they won't automatically inherit these event handlers.

Interactive Elements with jQuery

Here are the interactive elements with jQuery:

- **Event Listeners**: Readers will gain experience in adding event listeners to interactive elements within our project, such as the submit button for adding items and the delete buttons for removing items. We'll utilize event delegation to handle these events efficiently.
- **Dynamic Updates**: jQuery will be used to dynamically update the list when items are added or removed. This ensures that the user interface is always in sync with the underlying data.

- **User Feedback**: We'll implement feedback mechanisms to inform users of successful item additions and removals. This can include visual cues or informative messages.
- **Validation**: We'll add basic input validation to ensure that users don't submit empty or invalid items. jQuery will be instrumental in performing these checks.

Learning Outcomes

Learners will have created a fully functional dynamic list with interactive elements using jQuery. They will have gained practical experience in:

- Creating interactive web features with jQuery.
- Adding and removing elements dynamically.
- Handling user interactions with event listeners.
- Using CSS for styling and layout.
- Implementing basic input validation.

This project serves as a valuable hands-on experience, allowing readers to apply the concepts learned in previous chapters to a real-world scenario. It's an excellent opportunity to reinforce jQuery skills and build confidence in developing interactive web applications.

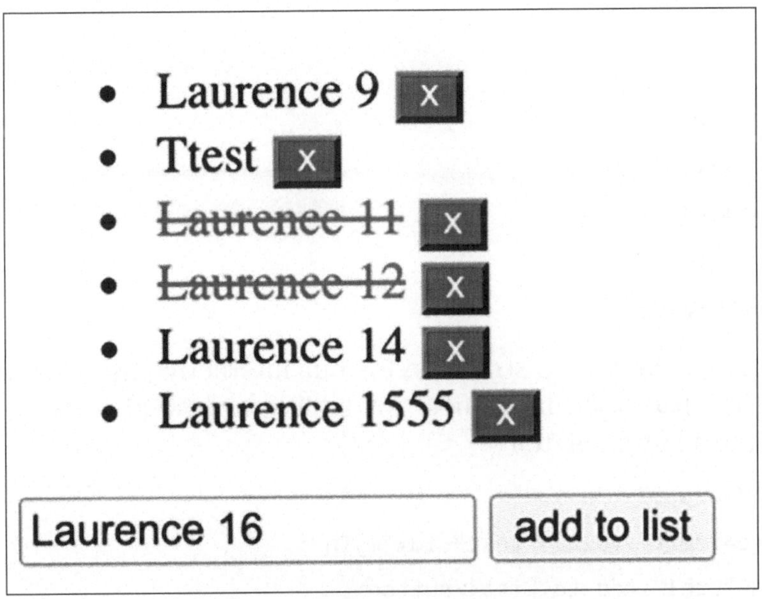

Figure 6.1: *Interactive list using jQuery*

Exercise: Create an Interactive List with jQuery

In this exercise, we'll build an interactive list using jQuery. Users will be able to add new items to the list, cross out items by clicking on them, and remove items by clicking a button associated with each item. Here are the steps:

Step 1: Styling the List Elements

We start by defining the CSS styles for our list elements. This includes styling for list items, the text decoration for crossed-out items, and the appearance of the delete buttons:

```
li span {
  padding: 5px;
}

.red span {
  color: red;
  text-decoration: line-through;
}

li button {
  font-size: 0.5em;
  background-color: red;
  color: white;
}
```

Step 2: HTML Structure

Next, we create the HTML structure for our interactive list. This includes an unordered list (`<ul>`), an input field for adding new items, and a button for triggering the addition of items:

```
<ul class="output"></ul>
<input type="text" value="test" id="myIn">
<button id="btn1">Add to List</button>
```

Step 3: jQuery Event Handling

We add a click event to the **`Add to List`** button (**`#btn1`**) that will trigger the creation of a new list item:

```
$('#btn1').click(adder);
```

We also initialize a counter to keep track of the number of added items:

```
let counter = 0;
```

Step 4: Adding List Items

In the adder function, we retrieve the value from the input field and create a new list item. **`$('<li>')`**: This is a jQuery function call that creates a new jQuery object. The argument '**`<li>`**' is an HTML string representing a list item element (**`<li>`**):

```
const val = $('input').val();

const $li = $('<li>');
```

Then, we create a **`<span>`** element to hold the text of the list item and set its text content to the input value:

```
const $el = $('<span>').text(val);
```

Additionally, we create a delete button (**`<button>`**) with the text **`'X'`**:

```
const $btn = $('<button>').text('X');
```

Step 5: Toggle Class on Click

We add a click event handler to the **`<span>`** element. When the user clicks on it, the class **`'red'`** is toggled on the parent **`<li>`**. This class adds a red color and a line-through decoration to the text, simulating a crossed-out item:

```
$el.click(function(){

  $li.toggleClass('red');

});
```

Step 6: Remove Item on Button Click

We also add a click event handler to the delete button. When clicked, it removes the parent **`<li>`** element from the list:

```
$btn.click(function(){

  $li.remove();

});
```

Step 7: Appending Elements

Finally, we append the **`<span>`** and the delete button to the **`<li>`** element, and then we append the **`<li>`** element to the **`<ul>`** with the class **`'output'`**. This effectively adds the new item to the list:

```
$li.append($el).append($btn);
$('.output').append($li);
```

We increment the counter and update the input field with a new default value:

```
counter++;
const temp = `Laurence ${counter}`;
$('input').val(temp);
```

Step 8: Validation of input

`.trim()` is used to remove any leading or trailing whitespace from the input value.

A check is added to see if the trimmed value is an empty string (**`val === ''`**). If it is, the function shows an alert and returns early, preventing an empty list item from being added.

```
const val = $('input').val().trim(); // Use trim() to remove any leading
/trailing whitespace
if (val === '') {
        alert('Please enter some text.'); // Simple alert for empty input
        return; // Exit the function if input is empty
}
```

The exercise is now complete. Users can add, cross out, and remove items from the list using the interactive elements.

By working through this exercise, readers will gain practical experience in creating interactive web features with jQuery, manipulating the DOM based on user interactions, and styling elements using CSS classes. This project provides valuable hands-on experience for web development with jQuery.

Summary

In this exercise, you've learned how to create an interactive list using jQuery. Users can add new items to the list, cross out items by clicking on them, and remove items by clicking a delete button associated with each item. The exercise is broken down into several steps, including styling the list elements with CSS, setting up the HTML structure, and implementing jQuery event handling to create, modify, and delete list items.

Conclusion

This chapter has provided readers with a hands-on experience that reinforces their understanding of jQuery concepts. By guiding readers through the creation of a dynamic list with interactive elements, this chapter has demonstrated how to apply various jQuery methods to modify both the content and structure of the list. Readers have learned how to make their projects fully functional by adding event listeners to the interactive elements. Furthermore, we've explored the crucial role of CSS in styling the list and its elements, ensuring not only functionality but also a visually appealing design.

In the next chapter, we'll delve into CSS properties and element attributes using jQuery. You'll learn how to dynamically change the appearance of page elements with the `.css()` method, manipulate attributes with `.attr()`, and enhance interactivity by adding or removing classes using `.addClass()`, `.removeClass()`, and `.toggleClass()`. Within the next chapter, you'll be introduced to modifying element styles and attributes, making your web projects more dynamic and visually appealing.

Points to Remember

- **Styling with CSS:**

  To define CSS styles for list elements, use CSS selectors and properties.

  For example, you can use selectors such as `li`, `.red`, and `li` button to target specific elements.

  Define properties like color, text decoration, font size, background color, and padding to style the elements as desired.

- **HTML Structure:**

  Create the HTML structure using standard HTML tags.

  Include an unordered list (`<ul>`), an input field for adding items (`<input>`), and a button for triggering item addition (`<button>`).

  Assign appropriate IDs and classes to elements for easy selection and manipulation.

- **jQuery Event Handling:**

  Use jQuery to add event handlers to elements.

  For instance, to add a click event to the `Add to List` button (`#btn1`), use `$('#btn1').click(handlerFunction);`.

  Initialize a counter variable to keep track of added items. You can declare it like let counter = 0;.

- **Adding List Items:**

  Retrieve input field value using `$('input').val()`.

  Create a new list item (`<li>`) using `$('<li>')`.

  Create a `<span>` element to hold text using `$('<span>').text(textContent)`.

  Create a delete button (`<button>`) using `$('<button>').text('X')`.

- **Toggle Class on Click:**

  Add a click event handler to a `<span>` element, for example, `$span.click(clickHandler)`.

  Use `.toggleClass('red')` to toggle the `'red'` class on the parent `<li>` element.

- **Remove Item on Button Click:**

  Add a click event handler to the delete button, for example, `$btn.click(clickHandler)`.

  Inside the event handler, use `$li.remove()` to remove the parent `<li>` element from the list.

- **Appending Elements:**

  Append elements to each other using `.append()`, for example, `$li.append($span).append($btn)`.

  Append the resulting `<li>` element to the `<ul>` with the class `'output'` using `$('.output').append($li)`.

Multiple Choice Questions

1. What is the purpose of the **'red'** class in the provided CSS styles?

```
.red span {
  color: red;
  text-decoration: line-through;
}
```

   A. To set the background color of the list items

   B. To add a line-through decoration to crossed-out items

   C. To change the font size of list items

   D. To underline the text of list items

2. What does the click event on the delete button (**<button>**) do?

   A. It adds a new list item

   B. It removes the input field

   C. It removes the parent **<li>** element from the list

   D. It toggles the **'red'** class on list items

3. What triggers the creation of a new list item in the provided code?

   A. Clicking on the "`Add to List`" button

   B. Hovering over the list item

   C. Typing in the input field

   D. Refreshing the webpage

Answers

1. B) To add a line-through decoration to crossed-out items
2. C) It removes the parent **<li>** element from the list
3. A) Clicking on the "`Add to List`" button

CHAPTER 7
CSS Properties and Element Attributes

Introduction

In this chapter, we'll explore how to work with CSS properties and element attributes using jQuery. This knowledge is essential for dynamically modifying the appearance and behavior of web page elements.

Structure

In this chapter, we will discuss the following topics:

- Getting and setting CSS properties with jQuery
- Getting and setting element attributes with jQuery
- Retrieving and modifying element dimensions with jQuery

Getting and Setting CSS Properties with jQuery

Before we dive into manipulation, we'll briefly review how CSS properties determine the visual style of web page elements.

1. **Changing CSS Properties:** jQuery provides the `.css()` method, which allows us to change CSS properties of selected elements. For instance, we can change the background color, font size, or margins of elements.

Here's a basic example:

```
$('.element').css('background-color', 'blue');
```

2. **Advanced CSS Manipulation:** Readers will learn how to perform advanced CSS manipulations, such as animating properties or applying CSS changes conditionally based on user interactions.

Example: Changing Background Color on Button Click

CSS:

```
<style>
  .box {
    width: 100px;
    height: 100px;
    background-color: lightblue;
    transition: background-color 0.5s;
  }
</style>
```

HTML:

```
<div class="box"></div>
<button id="changeColor">Change Color</button>
```

JS:

```
  $('#changeColor').click(function () {
    $('.box').css('background-color', 'lightcoral');
  });
```

Explanation:

In this example, we have a div element with the class `.box`. Initially, it has a light blue background color. When the Change Color button is clicked, the jQuery `.css()` method is used to change the background color of the .box element to light coral. The transition property in CSS provides a smooth color transition effect.

Getting and Setting Element Attributes with jQuery

Understanding Element Attributes: We'll explore the concept of element attributes, which are values that provide additional information about HTML elements, like href for links or **`src`** for images.

- **Using `.attr()`**: jQuery's **`.attr()`** method allows us to get or set attributes of selected elements. For example, we can change the src attribute of an image dynamically:

  ```
  $('img').attr('src', 'new-image.jpg');
  ```

- **Manipulating Attributes**: We'll demonstrate how to manipulate various attributes, including **`href`**, **`data-*`**, and custom attributes. Readers will learn how to create interactive elements by changing attributes based on user actions.

Example: Toggle Image Source

HTML

```
<img id="myImage" src="image1.jpg" alt="Image 1">
<button id="toggleImage">Toggle Image</button>
```

JS:

```
$('#toggleImage').click(function () {
  const image = $('#myImage');
  const currentSrc = image.attr('src');

  if (currentSrc === 'image1.jpg') {
    image.attr('src', 'image2.jpg');
    image.attr('alt', 'Image 2');
  } else {
    image.attr('src', 'image1.jpg');
    image.attr('alt', 'Image 1');
  }
});
```

Explanation:

In this example, we have an image element (`<img>`) with the id of `myImage`. Initially, it displays "`Image 1`" with the source attribute (src) set to "`image1.jpg`."

When the "`Toggle Image`" button is clicked, the jQuery `.attr()` method is used to:

Get the current value of the `src` attribute using `image.attr('src')` and store it in the `currentSrc` variable.

Check the current source (`currentSrc`).

If the current source is "`image1.jpg`," it changes the `src` attribute to "`image2.jpg`" and updates the alt attribute to "`Image 2`." Otherwise, it reverts to "`image1.jpg`" and "`Image 1`."

This example demonstrates how to use the `.attr()` method to dynamically change attributes of HTML elements based on user interactions, such as toggling between different images.

Retrieving and Modifying Element Dimensions with jQuery

Understanding Element Dimensions: We'll discuss the concept of element dimensions, including width, height, and positioning.

- **Using `.width()`, `.height()`, and `.position()`**: jQuery provides methods like `.width()` and `.height()` to retrieve and modify dimensions, as well as .position() to get the position of an element within its parent container. Examples will illustrate how to adjust the size and placement of elements.
- **Dynamic Layout Adjustments**: Readers will learn how to create responsive designs by dynamically adjusting element dimensions based on browser window size or user interactions.

Adding and Removing CSS Classes with jQuery:

Adding and Removing CSS Classes: We'll delve into the `.addClass()` and `.removeClass()` methods in jQuery, which allow us to add or remove CSS classes from selected elements. These classes can define various styles, making it easy to change an element's appearance with a single method call.

Example: Toggle CSS Classes on Button Click

CSS:

```
.red {
  color: red;
}
.blue {
  color: blue;
}
```

HTML:

```
<p id="myText">This text can change color.</p>
<button id="toggleRed">Toggle Red</button>
<button id="toggleBlue">Toggle Blue</button>
```

JS:

```
$('#toggleRed').click(function () {
  $('#myText').addClass('red'); // Add the 'red' class
  $('#myText').removeClass('blue'); // Remove the 'blue' class
});

$('#toggleBlue').click(function () {
  $('#myText').addClass('blue'); // Add the 'blue' class
  $('#myText').removeClass('red'); // Remove the 'red' class
});
```

Explanation:

In this example, we have a paragraph element (`<p>`) with the id of `myText`. Initially, it has no CSS classes applied, so its text color is the default.

We also have two buttons, "`Toggle Red`" and "`Toggle Blue`."

When the "`Toggle Red`" button is clicked, jQuery's `.addClass('red')` method is used to add the red class to `#myText`, changing its text color to red. Then, `.removeClass('blue')` is used to remove the blue class if it's present, ensuring that only the red class is applied.

Conversely, when the "`Toggle Blue`" button is clicked, jQuery's `.addClass('blue')` method is used to add the blue class to `#myText`, changing its text color to blue. `.removeClass('red')` is used to remove the red class if it's present, ensuring that only the blue class is applied.

These examples demonstrate how to use the `.addClass()` and `.removeClass()` methods to dynamically change the styling of HTML elements by toggling CSS classes based on user interactions.

Using `.toggleClass()`: The `.toggleClass()` method toggles a class on and off for selected elements. This is useful for creating interactive elements that change style with user interactions.

Exercise: Get the Style Properties of an Element

HTML:

```
<button id="btn1">Button 1</button>

<button id="btn2">Button 2</button>

<div></div>

<div></div>
```

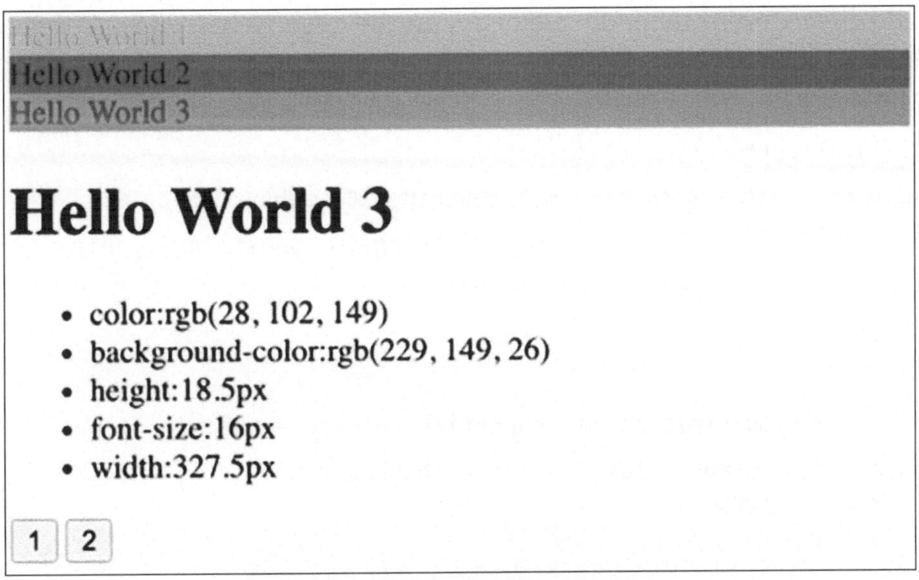

Figure 7.1: *Style properties of an element*

In this exercise, we'll explore how to interact with the style properties of HTML elements using jQuery. We'll add events to buttons and elements to update style properties, generate random colors, retrieve style properties, and increment the width of elements.

Step 1: Toggling Classes and Updating Style Properties

We start by adding click events to two buttons, **`#btn1`** and **`#btn2`**. When clicked, these buttons will toggle the **`'red'`** and **`'blue'`** classes on all div elements, respectively. Additionally, they will update the width style property.

```
$('#btn1').click(() => {
  $('div').toggleClass('red');
  $('div').css('width', '100px');
});


$('#btn2').click(() => {
  $('div').toggleClass('blue');
  $('div').css('width', '+=50');
});
```

Step 2: Generating Random Colors and Updating Style Properties

We add a click event to all div elements on the page. When clicked, this event generates random colors for the color and background-color style properties using JavaScript code.

```
$('div').click(function () {
  const rc = '#' + Math.random().toString(16).substring(2, 8);
  const rc2 = '#' + Math.random().toString(16).substring(2, 8);
  $(this).css('background-color', rc);
  $(this).css('color', rc2);

  // Retrieve multiple style properties and store them in 'temp'.
  const temp = $(this).css(['color', 'background-color', 'height',
'font-size', 'width']);

  // Create an HTML string to display the style properties.
  let elText = $(this).text();
```

```
  let html = `<h1>${elText}</h1><ul>`;
  for (const prop in temp) {
    html += `<li>${prop}:${temp[prop]}</li>`;
  }
  html += '</ul>';

  // Display the style properties in one of the page elements.
  output(html);
});
```

Step 3: Output Function

We create an output function to display content within one of the page elements **(.div4)**.

```
function output(val) {
  $('.div4').html(val);
}
```

Step 4: Testing

The exercise is complete, and users can interact with the buttons to toggle classes and update style properties, click on div elements to change their colors and retrieve style properties, and click **.div4** to display content.

By working through this exercise, readers will gain practical experience in using jQuery to update and retrieve style properties of HTML elements. They will also learn how to generate random colors, toggle classes, and dynamically adjust element dimensions. These skills are valuable for creating dynamic and visually appealing web applications.

Exercise: Getting and Setting Element Attributes with jQuery

In this exercise, we will work with input checkboxes and various attributes to understand how to get and set element properties. We'll also explore event handling and detaching elements for later use.

Instructions:

Using a for loop, create checkboxes with attributes. Add a click event to each checkbox that will output the value of the element from the attribute of "**`checked`**," the property of "**`checked`**," and using the **`is`** method for the **`checked`** state. Then, the output results to the page.

Using another loop, create some input checkbox elements, and then using the **`prop()`** method, set the checked Boolean value. Add a click event to track and output the checked results.

Add a click event to an element. Update the value by counting the clicks on that element.

Using the **`detach()`** method, remove an element and save it into a global variable. Then, on a separate event, append the stored detached element to the page again. Note that the events and properties will still be contained within that element.

CSS:

```
.red {
    color: red;
    font-size: 0.9em;
}

.blue {
    background-color: blue;
}

.box {
    width: 200px;
    height: 35px;
    border: 1px solid #ddd;
}
```

HTML:

```
<div class="div1">Hello World 1</div>
<div class="div2">Hello World 2</div>
<div class="div3" id="div3">Hello World 3</div>
```

```
<div class="div4">Laurence Svekis</div>
<input>
<button id="btn1">1</button>
<button id="btn2">2</button>
```

JavaScript Code:

```
let counter = 0;
const arr = [];

for (let i = 0; i < 5; i++) {
    $('<input>').attr({
        type: 'checkbox',
        value: i,
        checked: 'checked'
    }).appendTo('.div3').click(function () {
        checkerInput($(this));
    });
}

for (let i = 0; i < 5; i++) {
    $ele = $('<input>');
    $ele.attr({
        type: 'checkbox',
        value: i
    }).appendTo('.div4');
    $ele.prop('checked', true);
    $ele.click(function () {
        checkerInput($(this));
    });
}

function checkerInput($el) {
    let temp = '';
    temp += `<div>Attr : ${$el.attr('checked')}</div>`;
```

```
    temp += `<div>Prop : ${$el.prop('checked')}</div>`;
    temp += `<div>Is : ${$el.is(':checked')}</div>`;
    $('.div1').html(temp);
}

$('.div2').click(function () {
    counter++;
    $('.div1').html(`<div>Counter ${counter}</div>`);
});

$('.div2').click(function () {
    console.log($(this).attr('id'));
    const ran = Math.floor(Math.random() * 100);
    $(this).attr('id', `id${ran}`);
});

$('#btn1').click(() => {
    if (arr.length > 0) {
        $ele = arr.shift();
        $('.div4').append($ele);
    }
    $('input').attr({
        type: 'number',
        min: '0',
        max: '10',
        value: '5'
    });
});

$('#btn2').click(() => {
    $ele = $('.div1').detach();
    arr.push($ele);
});
```

In this exercise, you'll work with checkboxes, attributes, and element manipulation to better understand how to use jQuery for these tasks.

Please note that the second set of HTML checkboxes will return undefined for the checked option as the attribute checked: `'checked'` is not in the object.

Exercise: Get the Dimensions of Page Elements with jQuery Methods

In this exercise, we will explore how to get the dimensions and properties of page elements using jQuery. You will add a class to page elements and use event handlers to display various dimensions and properties when elements are clicked. Additionally, you will use buttons to display window and document height and width values in the console.

Instructions:

1. Add a class to the page elements to apply some common styling.
2. Add a click event to the div elements on the page. When an element is clicked, display within that element the following dimensions and properties:
   - Width
   - Height
   - Inner Width
   - Inner Height
   - Outer Width
   - Outer Height
   - Outer Width (including margins)
   - Outer Height (including margins)
3. Add a click event to the button with the id "`btn1`" to display in the console the following window and document dimensions:
   - Document Width
   - Window Width
   - Document Height
   - Window Height

CSS

```
.box {
    width: 200px;
    border: 5px solid #ddd;
    padding: 20px;
    margin: 10px;
}
```

HTML

```
<div class="div1">Hello World 1</div>
<div class="div2">Hello World 2</div>
<div class="div3" id="div3">Hello World 3</div>
<div class="div4">Laurence Svekis</div>
<input>
<button id="btn1">1</button>
```

JavaScript Code

```
$('div').addClass('box').click(function () {
    let html = `<div>Width : ${$(this).width()}</div>`;
    html += `<div>Height : ${$(this).height()}</div>`;
    html += `<div>Inner Width : ${$(this).innerWidth()}</div>`;
    html += `<div>Inner Height : ${$(this).innerHeight()}</div>`;
    html += `<div>Outer Width : ${$(this).outerWidth()}</div>`;
    html += `<div>Outer Height : ${$(this).outerHeight()}</div>`;
    html += `<div>Outer Width (incl. margins) : ${$(this).outer-
Width(true)}</div>`;
    html += `<div>Outer Height (incl. margins) : ${$(this).outerHe-
ight(true)}</div>`;
    $(this).html(html);
});

$('#btn1').click(() => {
    console.log(`Document Width: ${$(document).width()}px`);
    console.log(`Window Width: ${$(window).width()}px`);
```

```
    console.log(`Document Height: ${$(document).height()}px`);
    console.log(`Window Height: ${$(window).height()}px`);
});
```

In this exercise, you'll learn how to retrieve and display various dimensions and properties of HTML elements using jQuery, enhancing your understanding of how to interact with the DOM.

Conclusion

In this chapter, we explored the power of jQuery in manipulating the appearance and attributes of web elements. We also understood how to use various jQuery methods to modify CSS properties, such as changing background colors with **`.css()`**. Additionally, we also learned the techniques for getting and setting element attributes using **`.attr()`**, adding or removing CSS classes with **`.addClass()`** and **`.removeClass()`**, and toggling classes on and off with **`.toggleClass()`**.

We also learned how to navigate and select specific page elements with precision. In the next chapter, we will cover techniques such as using **`.find()`** to select descendant elements, **`.closest()`** to find the nearest matching ancestor, **`.next()`** and **`.prev()`** to choose sibling elements, and **`.filter()`** to refine selections based on conditions. You'll also discover how to select elements based on their visibility and state using :visible and :hidden selectors.

Multiple Choice Questions

1. Which jQuery method is used to modify the appearance of page elements by changing their CSS properties?

   a) `.text()`

   b) `.addClass()`

   c) `.css()`

   d) `.attr()`

2. How can you set the value of a selected attribute for an element using jQuery?

   a) `.attr()`

   b) `.css()`

   c) `.addClass()`

   d) `.toggleClass()`

3. What is the purpose of the **`.addClass()`** method in jQuery?

   a) To remove a class from selected elements

   b) To toggle a class on and off for selected elements

   c) To add a class to selected elements

   d) To retrieve the CSS properties of selected elements

4. Which jQuery method is used to toggle a class on and off for selected elements?

   a) `.toggleClass()`

   b) `.removeClass()`

   c) `.addClass()`

   d) `.attr()`

5. In jQuery, how can you modify the dimensions of an element?

   a) By using the `.css()` method

   b) By using the `.attr()` method

   c) By using the `.addClass()` method

   d) By using the `.toggleClass()` method

Answers

1. c) `.css()`
2. a) `.attr()`
3. c) To add a class to selected elements
4. a) `.toggleClass()`
5. a) By using the `.css()` method

CHAPTER 8

Traversing Page Elements

Introduction

In this chapter, we will explore advanced techniques for traversing and selecting page elements using jQuery. These methods allow you to navigate the DOM tree efficiently and select specific elements based on their relationships, attributes, and states.

Structure

In this chapter, we will cover the following topics:

- Traversing descendants of page elements with jQuery
- Traversing ancestors of page elements with jQuery
- Traversing siblings of page elements with jQuery
- Filtering page elements to select them with jQuery

Traversing Descendants of Page Elements with jQuery

In this section, we'll delve into the powerful `.find()` method in jQuery. This method allows you to traverse the DOM tree and select descendant elements of a selected element. This is particularly useful when you're dealing with complex HTML structures and you need to narrow down your selection to elements within a specific container or context.

Understanding `.find()`

Consider a scenario where you have a `<div>` with a class **`'container'`** that contains multiple `<p>` elements, and you want to change the text color of all those paragraphs to blue. Here's how you can use the method:

Example:

```
// Select all 'p' elements within a 'div' with the class 'container'
$('.container').find('p').css('color', 'blue');
```

In the preceding example:

a. **`$('.container')`** selects the **`<div>`** element with the class "**`container`**."

b. **`.find('p')`** traverses down the DOM tree to find all **`<p>`** elements that are descendants of the selected **`<div>`**.

c. **`.css('color', 'blue')`** sets the text color of all found **`<p>`** elements to blue.

Benefits of `.find()`:

- **Contextual Selection**: `.find()` allows you to work within a specific context or container, ensuring that you only affect the elements you intend to manipulate.
- **Nested Structures**: When dealing with nested HTML structures, **`.find()`** simplifies the process of selecting elements deeply nested within parent elements.
- **Efficient Traversal**: jQuery optimizes the traversal process, making it efficient even for complex DOM trees.
- **Chaining**: You can chain multiple jQuery methods together for more complex operations.

In summary, the **`.find()`** method is a valuable tool for selecting and manipulating descendant elements within a specified context, providing greater control and precision in your web development projects.

Exercise: Traversing Descendants of Page Elements with jQuery Selection

In this exercise, we will practice selecting an element and then navigating down to the descendants of the selected element using jQuery. You will learn how to access the children and descendants of a specific element and apply CSS styling to them.

Instructions:

1. Select an element with the class "**main**" and output its children into the console when the first button is clicked.
2. Add an event listener to the second button. When it is clicked, get the input value from the text field, and then search for that selector element within the "**main**" element. Apply a CSS style to the found elements (for example, change their color to blue).
3. When the third button is clicked, select all descendants of an element with the class "**main**" using the wildcard '*' and the find method. Apply CSS styling (for example, set their background color to purple).

CSS:

```
.box {
    width: 200px;
    border: 5px solid #ddd;
    padding: 20px;
    margin: 10px;
}
```

HTML:

```
<div class="main">
    <div class="div1">Hello World 1</div>
    <div class="div2"><span>Hello World 2</span></div>
    <div class="div3" id="div3">Hello World 3</div>
    <div class="div4">Laurence Svekis</div>
    <input>
    <div>
        <button id="btn1">1</button>
        <button id="btn2">2</button>
    </div>
    <button id="btn3">3</button>
</div>
```

```
JavaScript Code:
$('#btn1').click(() => {
    const children = $('.main').children();
    console.log(children);
});


$('#btn2').click(() => {
    const sel = $('input').val();
    if (sel) {
        console.log(sel);
        $('.main').find(sel).css('color', 'blue');
    }
});

$('#btn3').click(() => {
    $('.main div').find('*').css('background-color', 'purple');
});
```

In this exercise, you'll practice traversing the DOM to select children and descendants of a specific element within the page using jQuery, helping you become more proficient in manipulating and styling elements based on their relationships in the DOM hierarchy.

Each of the 3 buttons will perform a different action, interacting with the page elements.

Button 1 (**`#btn1`**) Click Event:

When the button with **`id="btn1"`** is clicked, the code retrieves all child elements of the div with the class main. It then logs these child elements to the console.

When the button with **`id="btn2"`** is clicked, the code first gets the value entered in the input field. If there is a value (**`sel`**), it searches within the **`div.main`** for elements that match the selector provided in the input field. It then changes the text color of these matched elements to blue. This allows dynamic selection based on the user's input. For example, if the user inputs .div1, the text color of the first div inside **`div.main`** will change to blue.

Clicking the button with **`id="btn3"`** affects every descendant of all div elements that are direct children of **`div.main`**. It finds all descendants (* selector) within these divs and changes their background color to purple.

Traversing Ancestors of Page Elements with jQuery

In this section, we'll explore the **`.closest()`** method in jQuery. This method allows you to traverse up the DOM tree and select the first ancestor element that matches a given selector. This is incredibly useful when you need to locate a specific parent element of an element, even if there are multiple levels of nesting in your HTML structure.

Understanding `.closest()`

Consider a scenario where you have an HTML structure with several nested **`<div>`** elements, and you want to select the nearest ancestor **`<div>`** element with the class "**`parent`**" when a specific element is clicked. Here's how you can achieve this using the **`.closest()`** method:

Example:

```
// Select the nearest ancestor 'div' with the class 'parent'
$('#myElement').closest('div.parent').css('border', '1px solid red');
```

In the preceding example:

1. **`$('#myElement')`** selects the target element with the id "**`myElement.`**"
2. **`.closest('div.parent')`** traverses up the DOM tree to find the nearest ancestor <div> element with the class "**`parent.`**"
3. **`.css('border', '1px solid red')`** applies a red border to the found ancestor element.

Benefits of `.closest()`

- **Targeted Selection**: **`.closest()`** helps you pinpoint a specific ancestor element that matches the provided selector, even if there are multiple levels of nesting in your HTML.
- **Cleaner Code**: It simplifies code compared to manually traversing the DOM tree with multiple **`.parent()`** calls.

- **Maintainability**: Makes your code more maintainable and less prone to breaking when the structure of your HTML changes.
- **Efficiency**: jQuery optimizes the traversal process, ensuring quick and efficient selection of ancestor elements.

In summary, the `.closest()` method is a valuable tool for selecting the nearest ancestor element that meets your criteria, simplifying complex DOM tree navigation and enhancing the precision of your element selections.

Traversing Siblings of Page Elements with jQuery

In this section, we'll explore the `.next()` and `.prev()` methods in jQuery, which are used to select the next or previous sibling elements of a given element. These methods enable you to perform actions on adjacent elements in the DOM tree, which can be especially useful when you need to manipulate elements that share the same parent.

Understanding `.next()` and `.prev()`

Consider a scenario where you have a list of elements and you want to highlight the element following a specific element with the class "**`selected`**" when a certain condition is met. Here's how you can use the `.next()` method:

Example:

```
// Select the next sibling element of a 'div' with the class 'selected'
$('.selected').next().addClass('highlighted');
```

In the preceding example:

1. **`$('.selected')`** selects the element with the class "**`selected.`**"
2. **`.next()`** selects the next sibling element in the DOM, which is then highlighted by adding the "**`highlighted`**" class.
3. Similarly, you can use **`.prev()`** to select the previous sibling element.

Benefits of `.next()` and `.prev()`:

- **Precise Selection**: These methods allow you to precisely target elements that are adjacent to a specific element, simplifying complex DOM interactions.
- **Sequential Actions**: You can easily perform sequential actions on elements within the same parent container.

- **Readable Code**: Code readability is improved, as the intention of selecting adjacent elements is clear.
- **Efficient Traversal**: jQuery optimizes the traversal process, making it efficient for navigating sibling elements.

In summary, the `.next()` and `.prev()` methods are valuable for selecting and interacting with sibling elements in the DOM, enabling you to create dynamic and responsive web pages with ease.

Exercise: Traversing Siblings Page Elements and Other Selections with jQuery

In this exercise, you will work with various sibling methods in jQuery to traverse elements at the same level as siblings of the selected element. You will apply different classes to these elements to see the effects of the traversal methods.

Instructions:

1. Apply a class of "**`box`**" to all siblings of the selected element when the first button is clicked.
2. Add an event listener to the second button to remove all elements with the class "**`box`**" when clicked.
3. When the third button is clicked, add a class of "**`box`**" to siblings of an element that have a tag name of "`div`."
4. On a button click, use the **`next()`**, **`nextAll()`**, and **`nextUntil()`** methods on page elements and apply classes to the selected elements.
5. On another button click, use the **`prev()`**, **`prevAll()`**, and **`prevUntil()`** methods on page elements and apply classes to the matching elements.

CSS

```
.box {
    border: 1px solid #ddd;
    padding: 5px;
    color: red;
}

.box1 {
    border: 1px solid #ddd;
```

```
        padding: 5px;
        color: blue;
    }

    .box2 {
        border: 1px solid #ddd;
        padding: 5px;
        color: green;
    }
```

HTML:

```
<nav>
    <div class="main">
        <div xclass="div1">Hello World 1</div>
        <div class="div2"><span>Hello World 2</span></div>
        <div class="div3" id="div3">Hello World 3</div>
        <div class="div4">Laurence Svekis</div>
        <input>
        <button id="btn1">1</button>
        <button id="btn2">2</button>
        <button id="btn3">3</button>
        <span>Hello</span>
    </div>
</nav>
<button id="btn4">4</button>
<button id="btn5">5</button>
```

JavaScript Code:

```
$('#btn1').click(() => {
    const siblings = $('#btn1').siblings();
    console.log(siblings);
    siblings.addClass('box');
});
```

```
$('#btn2').click(() => {
    $('.box').removeClass('box');
});

$('#btn3').click(() => {
    $('#btn1').siblings('div').addClass('box');
});

$('#btn4').click(() => {
    $('#btn1').next().addClass('box');
    $('#btn1').nextAll('span').addClass('box');
    $('#div3').nextUntil('button').addClass('box1');
});

$('#btn5').click(() => {
    $('#btn1').prev().addClass('box2');
    $('#btn1').prevAll('span').addClass('box2');
    $('#div3').prevUntil('button').addClass('box2');
});
```

This exercise helps you become more familiar with jQuery's sibling traversal methods and demonstrates how to apply them to elements on the same level in the DOM hierarchy. You'll be able to see how different methods work in selecting and manipulating sibling elements.

Filtering Page Elements to Select them with jQuery

In this section, we'll dive into the `.filter()` method in jQuery. This method allows you to refine a selection based on a given condition, enabling you to select elements that meet specific criteria within a larger set of elements. This is incredibly useful when you want to narrow down your selection to elements that match certain conditions.

Understanding `.filter()`

Consider a scenario where you have a list of tasks represented by `<li>` elements, and you want to select and add a **"`completed-task`"** class to those tasks that contain the text "**completed**." Here's how you can achieve this using the **.filter()** method:

Example:

```
// Select all 'li' elements containing the text 'completed'
$('li').filter(function () {
  return $(this).text() === 'completed';
}).addClass('completed-task');
```

In the preceding example:

a. **$('li')** selects all **<li>** elements on the page.

b. **.filter(function () {...})** applies a filter to the selection, evaluating the provided function for each element.

c. **return $(this).text() === 'completed';** checks if the text content of each <li> element equals "completed."

d. **.addClass('completed-task')** adds the "completed-task" class to elements that meet the filter condition.

Benefits of .filter():

- **Selective Targeting**: **.filter()** allows you to selectively target elements within a larger set based on specific conditions, making your selection more precise.
- **Dynamic Filtering**: You can dynamically filter elements based on changing conditions or user interactions.
- **Readability**: Code readability is enhanced because the filter condition is clearly defined within the function.
- **Efficiency**: jQuery optimizes the filtering process, ensuring efficient selection of elements.

In summary, the **.filter()** method is a powerful tool for refining your element selection based on specific conditions or criteria, giving you fine-grained control over the elements you manipulate on your web page.

Selecting Elements Based on Visibility and State

In this section, we'll explore how to select elements in jQuery based on their visibility using the **:visible** and **:hidden** selectors. These selectors are incredibly useful for targeting elements that are currently displayed or hidden on a web page, allowing you to apply specific actions or styles to them.

Understanding `:visible` and `:hidden`

Consider a scenario where you have a webpage with multiple **`<div>`** elements, some of which are visible and others hidden. You want to select all the visible **`<div>`** elements and change their background color to green. Here's how you can do it using the `:visible` selector:

Example:

```
// Select all visible 'div' elements
$('div:visible').css('background-color', 'green');
```

In the preceding example:

a. **`$('div:visible')`** selects all **`<div>`** elements that are currently visible on the page.

b. **`.css('background-color', 'green')`** changes the background color of the selected visible **`<div>`** elements to green.

c. You can similarly use **`:hidden`** to select elements that are currently hidden.

Benefits of :visible and :hidden:

- **Visibility Control**: These selectors are invaluable for interacting with elements based on their current visibility state.
- **Dynamic Handling**: You can dynamically respond to changes in element visibility, making your website more interactive.
- **Efficiency**: jQuery efficiently identifies visible and hidden elements, optimizing performance.
- **User Experience**: Using these selectors, you can enhance the user experience by applying different styles or actions based on what the user can see.

In summary, the `:visible` and `:hidden` selectors in jQuery are powerful tools for selecting elements based on their visibility, enabling you to create responsive and dynamic web pages that adapt to user interactions and content changes.

Exercise: Dynamic Page Elements with jQuery

In this exercise, you will learn how to create dynamic page elements using jQuery. You'll start with an array of string values and use jQuery to loop through these items and generate dynamic content on the page.

Instructions:

1. Create an array of string values containing names.
2. Use the `$.each()` method to loop through the array items. In the callback function, add each value as a `<div>` element to the page and assign it a class of "`box.`"
3. Select all elements with a class of "`box`" and use the `each()` method again to iterate through them.
4. For each "`box`" element, select its text content using the `text()` method and store it as a variable.
5. Empty the contents of the "`box`" element using the `empty()` method.
6. Create a `<span>` element with the text content you stored in step 4 and append it to the "`box`" element.
7. Add two buttons, one with the text "`Up`" and the other with the text "`Down`," to each "`box`" element.
8. Add a click event to the "`Up`" button. Inside the event handler, select the previous sibling of the parent element and assign it to a variable (`$sel`).
9. Check if the length of the selected element is greater than zero. If it is, add a class of "`active`" to the current "`box`" element and slide it up slowly. When the slide-up animation is complete, remove the "`active`" class, insert the "`box`" element before the selected element using `insertBefore()`, and slide it down fast.
10. Add a click event to the "`Down`" button. Inside the event handler, select the next sibling of the parent element and assign it to a variable (`$sel`).
11. Check if the length of the selected element is greater than zero. If it is, add a class of "`active`" to the current "`box`" element and slide it up slowly. When the slide-up animation is complete, remove the "`active`" class, insert the "`box`" element after the selected element using `insertAfter()`, and slide it down fast.
12. Apply some animations and styling to the "`box`" elements for better visual effects.

CSS:

```
.btn {
    background-color: black;
```

```
            color: white;
            font-size: 0.6em;
        }

        .output span {
            margin: 5px;
        }

        .active {
            color: red;
        }
```

HTML:

```
    <div class="output"></div>
```

JavaScript Code:

```
const arr = ['Laurence', 'Larry', 'Mike', 'Dave', 'Jane', 'Joe', 'Lisa',
'Jack'];

$.each(arr, (ind, val) => {
    let html = `${ind + 1} ${val}`;
    $('<div>').html(html).addClass('box').appendTo('.output');
});

$('.box').each(function () {
    $ele = $(this);
    $par = $ele.parent();
    const temp = $ele.text();
    $ele.empty();
    $('<span>').text(temp).appendTo($ele);
    $btn1 = $('<button>').text('Up').addClass('btn').appendTo($ele);
    $btn2 = $('<button>').text('Down').addClass('btn').appendTo($ele);
```

```
    $btn1.click(function () {
        $sel = $(this).parent().prev();
        if ($sel.length > 0) {
            $(this).parent().addClass('active');
            $(this).parent().slideUp('slow', function () {
                $(this).removeClass('active');
                $(this).insertBefore($sel);
                $(this).slideDown('fast');
            });
        }
    });

    $btn2.click(function () {
        $sel = $(this).parent().next();
        if ($sel.length > 0) {
            $(this).parent().addClass('active');
            $(this).parent().slideUp('slow', function () {
                $(this).removeClass('active');
                $(this).insertAfter($sel);
                $(this).slideDown('fast');
            });
        }
    });
});
```

This exercise demonstrates how to dynamically create page elements, manipulate their content, and add interactivity to them using jQuery. It's a practical example of creating and managing dynamic content on a web page.

Conclusion

This chapter has equipped you with advanced jQuery techniques for precisely traversing and selecting page elements. We learned to navigate the DOM tree, select descendants with **`.find()`**, find ancestors with **`.closest()`**, choose siblings with **`.next()`** and **`.prev()`**, and refine selections using **`.filter()`**. We also explored selecting elements based on visibility and state using **`:visible`** and

`:hidden` selectors. These skills empower you to create dynamic and interactive web applications.

In the next chapter, we'll explore two key jQuery methods that enhance your work with page elements. First, the **`data()`** method lets you attach and retrieve custom data associated with elements, making it ideal for storing state or metadata. Second, the **`index()`** method allows you to pinpoint an element's position among its siblings, enabling precise operations within lists or groups.

Multiple Choice Questions

1. Which jQuery method is used to select descendant elements of a selected element that match a given selector?

   a) `.find()`

   b) `.next()`

   c) `.closest()`

   d) `.filter()`

2. What does the `.next()` method in jQuery allow you to select?

   a) Descendant elements

   b) Ancestor elements

   c) Sibling elements

   d) Elements based on their visibility

3. Which jQuery method is used to select descendant elements of a chosen element within the DOM?

   a) `.find()`

   b) `.prev()`

   c) `.filter()`

   d) `.next()`

4. How can you refine a selection based on a given condition using jQuery?
    a) `.next()`
    b) `.filter()`
    c) `.closest()`
    d) `.prev()`
5. Which jQuery selector is used to select elements that are currently hidden on a web page?
    a) `:visible`
    b) `:hidden`
    c) `.find()`
    d) `.next()`

Answers

1. a) `.find()`
2. c) Sibling elements
3. a) `.find()`
4. b) `.filter()`
5. b) `:hidden`

Chapter 9

jQuery Data and Element Index Method

Introduction

This chapter covers two important methods that enable developers to work more efficiently with page elements: the jQuery `data()` method and the `index()` method. The `data()` method allows developers to attach custom data to an element and retrieve it later on. This can be useful for storing state information or metadata that is associated with an element. The chapter covers the basics of how to use the `data()` method to store and retrieve data associated with an element.

The `index()` method, on the other hand, allows developers to retrieve the index position of an element in relation to its siblings. This can be useful for performing operations on a specific element in a list or group of elements. The chapter covers how to use the `index()` method to get the position of an element, as well as techniques for using the `:eq()` and `:lt()` selectors to select elements based on their position in relation to others.

By the end of this chapter, readers will have a solid understanding of how to use the `data()` and `index()` methods to work more efficiently with page elements in jQuery.

Structure

In this chapter, we will cover the following topics:

- Saving values into the element object with the jQuery data method
- Find the position of a specific element within a set of elements by using the `.index()` method. This method returns the index value of the selected element, indicating its position relative to its siblings
- Getting the jQuery elements as DOM elements with the jQuery toArray method

Saving values into the element object with the jQuery data method

In this chapter, we dive into two crucial methods in jQuery that allow developers to enhance their efficiency when working with web elements. We'll explore the **`data()`** method and the **`index()`** method, unveiling their capabilities and real-world applications.

jQuery Data Method `.data()`

The `data()` method empowers developers to attach custom data to HTML elements and retrieve that data when needed.

Saving values into the element object with jQuery's **`.data()`** method is a fundamental concept in web development. This method allows you to attach custom data to HTML elements, which can be particularly useful for a wide range of applications. Let's explore how you can use the **`.data()`** method to save values into the element object and understand why it's a valuable tool.

Saving Values with `.data()`

The `.data()` method in jQuery attaches additional information to DOM elements without altering the DOM structure or the element's presentation in the source code. You can store any kind of data, such as strings, numbers, objects, or arrays, within an element. Here's how you save values into an element's data:

```
$('#myElement').data('key', 'value');
```

In this example, we associate the string value with the key in the `#myElement` element.

You can store data in an element using the **`.data()`** method. To do this, you typically select the element you want to associate data with and call **`.data('key', 'value')`**, where 'key' is a unique identifier for your data, and 'value' is the data you want to store.

```
$('#myElement').data('userInfo', { name: 'Laurence', age: 40, email:
'laurence@example.com' });
```

In this example, we've associated an object with the key `userInfo` to the HTML element with the ID `myElement`.

Retrieving Data

To retrieve the stored data, you can use the **`.data()`** method again, but this time, you don't provide a value. You simply provide the **`'key'`** to retrieve the data associated with that key.

```
const userData = $('#myElement').data('userInfo');
```

Now, the userData variable will contain the object we stored earlier, allowing you to access properties like name, age, and email.

Removing Data

You can also remove data associated with an element by calling **`.removeData('key')`.**

```
$('#myElement').removeData('userInfo');
```

This will remove the `userInfo` data associated with the element.

Benefits of using **`.data()`** are:

- It keeps data easily readable and separate from HTML.
- It manages data with element and retrieves it when needed.
- It shares data making it easier to manage.
- You can store various types of data.
- Data can be handled better within events and event-specific information.

Exercise data() example

The following code example is a jQuery exercise that demonstrates how to store and retrieve the value of the text content from clicked elements using the jQuery `data()` method. The exercise has the following steps:

1. Add a click event to all the divs: In this step, a click event is attached to all div elements within the `.main` container. Whenever one of these div elements is clicked, a function is executed.
2. When the div is clicked, get the current **`text()`** value and store it in the **`data():`** Inside the click event function, the current text value of the clicked div element is obtained using **`$(this).text()`**. This value is then stored using the **`data()`** method. The key for the data is set to `past`, and the value is the text content.
3. Update the **`text()`** of the element: After storing the text content in the data, the text of the clicked div element is updated. In this exercise, the text is updated to include a counter that keeps track of how many times the div has been clicked. The text is modified to display the text content plus the counter.
4. Add events to the buttons to use the data value of the element and output the **`data()`** value as the new **`text()`** of the element: There are several buttons (**`btn1, btn2`**, **`btn3, btn4`**) provided in the HTML. Each button corresponds to a specific div element. When a button is clicked, it retrieves the stored data using **`.data('past'),`** which was previously stored when the associated div was clicked. The retrieved value is then set as the new text content of the corresponding div.

HTML Code

```
<nav>

<div class="main">

<div class="div1">Hello World 1</div>

<div class="div2"><span>Hello World 2</span></div> <div class="div3"
id="div3">Hello World 3</div>

<div class="div4">Laurence Svekis</div>

<input>

<button id="btn1">1</button>

<button id="btn2">2</button>
```

```
<button id="btn3">3</button>
<span>Hello</span>
</div>
</nav>
<button id="btn4">4</button>
<button id="btn5">5</button>
```

JavaScript Code

```
let counter = 0;
let temp = '';
$('input').val('Laurence Svekis');
$('.main div').click(function(){
$(this).data('past',$(this).text()); counter++;
const temp = $('input').val();
const html = `${temp} Counter : ${counter}`; $(this).html(html);
})
$('#btn1').click(()=>{
const val = $('.div1').data('past'); $('.div1').text(val);
console.log(val);
})
$('#btn2').click(()=>{
const val = $('.div2').data('past'); $('.div2').text(val);
console.log(val);
})
$('#btn3').click(()=>{
const val = $('.div3').data('past'); $('.div3').text(val);
console.log(val);
})
$('#btn4').click(()=>{
const val = $('.div4').data('past');

$('.div4').text(val);
console.log(val);
})
```

The counter variable is initialized to keep track of how many times a div is clicked, and temp is also initialized but not used in this context.

The value of the input field is set to `Laurence Svekis`.

The click event is attached to all div elements within the .main container. When clicked, the text content of the div is stored in its data as "**`past`**," and the text content is updated to include the counter.

For each button (**`btn1, btn2, btn3, btn4`**), a click event is attached. When a button is clicked, the stored data value for the corresponding div is retrieved and set as the new text content of that div. Additionally, the retrieved value is logged to the console.

In summary, this code provides a practical exercise to learn how to store and retrieve data from elements and apply it to create interactive elements that keep track of user interactions. It showcases the use of the **`data()`** method to save and retrieve data and how this data can be utilized to update the text content of elements dynamically.

Index of Page Element Index Method `.index()`

The **`index()`** method is your toolkit for determining an element's position in relation to its siblings. To use the **`index()`** method to get an element's position. The **`.index()`** method in jQuery is a powerful tool that allows you to get an element's position in relation to its siblings within a selected group of elements. This method is especially useful for identifying the position of an element within a list, a group of items, or any ordered collection. Let's explore how you can use the **`.index()`** method to get an element's position and leverage its functionalities.

Using `.index()`

The **`.index()`** method can be called on a specific element to retrieve its position among a set of elements. Here's how you can use it:

```
const position = $('#myElement').index();
```

In this example, position will contain the index of **`#myElement`** within the group of elements sharing the same parent.

Using `index()` in code:

```
<ol id="myList">
    <li>Item 1</li>
    <li>Item 2</li>
    <li>Item 3</li>
</ol>


$('#myList li').click(function() {
    const position = $(this).index();
    alert(`You clicked item ${position + 1}`);
});
```

In this example, when a list item is clicked, the code retrieves its position using **`.index()`** and shows an alert indicating the item's position.

Element Position

To find the position of a specific element, call **`.index()`** on that element. The method will return a zero-based index, indicating its position in the group.

Selecting elements based on their position relative to others is a common task when working with jQuery. Knowing how to identify and choose elements based on their relationship to neighboring elements can be very useful.

The **`index()`** method in jQuery allows you to retrieve the index position of an element in relation to its siblings. This can be very useful when you need to identify the specific position of an element within a group of similar elements.

The most basic usage of the **`index()`** method is to call it on a jQuery object. For example, if you have a set of sibling elements, you can call **`index()`** on one of them to get its position among its siblings.

```
// Assuming you have a set of sibling elements with the class item
const position = $('.item').index();
console.log(`Position: ${position}`);
```

This will log the position (0-based index) of the selected element among its siblings.

You can also use the **`index()`** method in combination with a selector to find the index of a specific element within a set of siblings that match the selector.

```
// Assuming you want to find the index of a specific element with the class active
const position = $('.item.active').index('.item');
console.log(`Position: ${position}`);
```

In this case, you're finding the index of the element with the class **active** within its siblings with the class item.

A common use case is to determine which element was clicked within a set of elements. You can use the **index()** method to find the index of the clicked element and then perform actions based on that index.

```
// Assuming you have a set of clickable elements with the class clickable
$('.clickable').click(function () {
  const position = $(this).index();
  console.log(`Clicked on item at position: ${position}`);
});
```

When a user clicks an element with the class **clickable,** this code logs the position of that element within the set of its siblings.

The **:eq()** and **:lt()** selectors are powerful tools in jQuery that allow you to pinpoint elements within a selection based on their index. They are extremely useful when you want to select specific elements from a set of matched elements.

Using the :eq() Selector:

The **:eq()** selector allows you to select a specific element within a set by providing its index. Indexing starts from 0.

For example, to select the second element within a set of elements, you would use **:eq(1)** because it is at index 1 (remember, the index is 0-based).

```
$('ul li:eq(2)').css('color', 'red');
```

In this case, the text color of the third **<li>** element (index 2) within a **<ul>** element is changed to red.

Using the :lt() Selector:

The **:lt()** selector allows you to select all elements up to, but not including, a specified index. This is useful when you want to select a range of elements within a set. To select the first three elements, you would use **:lt(3)**:

```
$('ul li:lt(3)').addClass('highlight');
```

This will add the **highlight** class to the first, second, and third **<li>** elements within a **<ul>**.

These selectors are helpful in situations where you want to target specific elements within a set without having to manually count elements in the DOM structure. They provide a concise and efficient way to work with elements based on their position within a selection, making your code more dynamic and flexible.

Exercise: Use the get() method to return the DOM element object

In this exercise, you will be using the **.get()** method in jQuery to retrieve DOM element objects from a selected set of elements. Once you have the DOM element object, you'll use JavaScript's DOM methods and properties to interact with these elements. Specifically, you will create a click event on buttons that will get the length of items in the jQuery selection and then loop through these items, using the **.get()** method to return the DOM element object and retrieve the `textContent` value from each element. Finally, you'll add the values to the page using jQuery.

Here are more detailed steps to follow for this exercise:

Step 1: Select a jQuery Set of Elements

- You'll start by selecting a set of elements using a jQuery selector. In your case, you're selecting elements with the class `main div`.

Step 2: Use the .get() Method and JavaScript DOM properties

- In the first button's click event (**#btn1**), you're using the **.get(1)** method for retrieving the DOM element object at index 1. This corresponds to the second element in the set (since the index is zero-based).
- You then use JavaScript DOM properties to interact with this element. You're logging its **innerHTML** and `textContent` values to the console.

Step 3: Create a Click Event to Loop Through Elements

- In the second button's click event (**#btn2**), you're performing a more complex operation.
- First, you get the length of the elements in the jQuery selection using **.length**.
- You then initialize an empty html variable to store the text content of elements.

- Next, you start a for loop to iterate through the elements. Inside the loop, you use the **.get(i)** method to retrieve the DOM element object at each index, and you log its `textContent` value to the console.
- You're also concatenating the index and `textContent` value into the html string.
- Finally, you're using jQuery to set the **text()** of an element with the class "**span1**" to display the concatenated `textContent` values.

This exercise demonstrates how to use the **.get()** method to access DOM element objects within a jQuery selection and utilize JavaScript's DOM properties to interact with those elements. By adding the `textContent` values to the page, you can display information from the DOM elements to the user in a different format or context.

HTML

```
<nav>
<div class="main">
<div class="div1">Hello World 1</div>
<div class="div2"><span>Hello World 2</span></div> <div class="div3" id="div3">Hello World 3</div>
<div class="div4">Laurence Svekis</div>
<input>
<button id="btn1">1</button>
<button id="btn2">2</button>
<button id="btn3">3</button>
<span class="span1">Hello</span>
</div>
</nav>
<button id="btn4">4</button>
<button id="btn5">5</button>
```

JavaScript

```
$('#btn1').click(()=>{
const temp = $('.main div').get(1);
console.log(temp.innerHTML);
console.log(temp.textContent);
})
```

```
$('#btn2').click(()=>{
const len = $('.main div').length;
console.log(len);
let html = '';
for(let i=0;i<len;i++){
const temp = $('.main div').get(i);
console.log(temp.textContent);
html += `${i}. ${temp.textContent} `;
}
$('.main .span1').text(html);
})
```

Exercise: Make a selection of page elements with jQuery and return the `index()` value of the selected element

This exercise focuses on using jQuery's **`index()`** method to return the index value of selected elements in different scenarios. It involves adding click events to elements and outputting their index values into the console. Here are the detailed steps for this exercise:

Step 1: Create a Button Click Event to Output Index

a. In this step, you're targeting the button with the id btn1 to create a click event.
b. When this button is clicked, you're using the **`$(this).index()`** method to retrieve the index of the clicked button.
c. You're logging the index value to the console.

Step 2: Add Click Events to Page Divs in the `main` Class

a. You're targeting all the div elements within the main class **`(.main div)`** using a selector.
b. For each of these divs, you're creating a click event.
c. Within the click event, you're obtaining the index value of the clicked div using **`$(this).index()`**.
d. You're also capturing the existing text content of the div with **`$(this).text()`**.

e. Then, you're updating the text content of the div to include both the index and the original text content (for example, **"1 Hello World 1"**).

f. This visually displays the index value alongside the existing text on the clicked div.

Step 3: Create a UL and Add LI Items with Click Events

a. You're creating an unordered list (**<ul>**) and prepending it to the nav element using **$('<ul>').prependTo('nav')**.

b. Inside a loop that runs ten times **(for(let i=0;i<10;i++))**, you're adding list items (**<li>**) to the unordered list.

c. Each list item contains text like **"0 List Item,"** **"1 List Item,"** and so on.

d. For each list item, you're attaching a click event.

e. Within the click event for the list items, you're using **$(this).index()** to retrieve the index of the clicked list item.

f. You're then logging this index to the console.

g. This allows you to determine and display the index of the clicked list item.

This exercise showcases how to use the **index()** method to obtain the index values of elements in various contexts. Whether it's a button, a div, or a list item, you're adding click events to interact with these elements and display their index values.

HTML

```
<nav>

<div class="main">

<div class="div1">Hello World 1</div>

<div class="div2"><span>Hello World 2</span></div> <div class="div3"
id="div3">Hello World 3</div>

<div class="div4">Laurence Svekis</div>

<input>

<button id="btn1">1</button>

<button id="btn2">2</button>

<button id="btn3">3</button>

<span class="span1">Hello</span>

</div>
```

```
</nav>
<button id="btn4">4</button>
<button id="btn5">5</button>
```

JavaScript

```
$('#btn1').click(function(){
console.log($(this).index());
})
$('.main div').click(function(){
const val = $(this).index();
const temp = $(this).text();
$(this).text(`${val} ${temp}`);
})
const $ul = $('<ul>').prependTo('nav');
for(let i=0;i<10;i++){
$('<li>').text(`${i} List
Item`).appendTo($ul).click(function(){
console.log($(this).index());
})
}
```

jQuery Data Method (`.data()`)

- The `data()` method allows developers to attach custom data to an HTML element and retrieve it later on.
- It's useful for storing state information or metadata associated with an element.
- You can store different types of data, such as strings, numbers, objects, or arrays, within an element.
- To save data into an element, you typically select the element and use `.data('key', 'value')`, where `'key'` is a unique identifier for the data, and `'value'` is the data you want to store.
- You can retrieve stored data by using `.data('key')`.
- The `removeData('key')` method is used to remove data associated with an element.

Index of Page Element Index Method (`.index()`):

- The **`index()`** method enables developers to retrieve the index position of an element in relation to its siblings.
- It's valuable for performing operations on a specific element within a list or group of elements.
- You can call **`.index()`** on a specific element to obtain its position among a set of elements.
- The index is a zero-based value, indicating the position within the selected group.
- You can use the **`:eq()`** and **`:lt()`** selectors to select elements based on their position within the group. **`:eq()`** selects a specific element by providing its index, while **`:lt()`** selects all elements up to a specified index.

Conclusion

The chapter covers how to use these methods and provides practical examples and exercises to demonstrate their usage. Readers will have a solid understanding of how to use the **`data()`** and **`index()`** methods to work efficiently with page elements in jQuery.

The next chapter focuses on event handling with jQuery, a fundamental aspect of developing interactive web applications. It delves into the event model in JavaScript and shows how jQuery can be used to bind and trigger events. Readers will explore various event methods in jQuery, such as **`.click()`**, **`.hover()`**, **`.submit()`**, and **`.keypress()`**, and learn how to apply them to manage user interactions on web pages.

Additionally, this chapter covers advanced event-handling techniques. Readers will discover how to use event delegation to handle events for dynamically created elements and how the **`.on()`** method can be employed to bind multiple events simultaneously. It also delves into event bubbling and propagation, as well as the use of event methods like **`.stopPropagation()`** and **`.preventDefault()`** to control event behavior effectively.

Multiple Choice Questions

1. What is the primary purpose of the jQuery `.data()` method?
   a) Styling HTML elements
   b) Attaching custom data to an HTML element
   c) Creating new HTML elements
   d) Parsing JSON data
2. Which of the following data types can be stored within an HTML element using `.data()`?
   a) Strings and numbers only
   b) Objects and arrays only
   c) Strings, numbers, objects, or arrays
   d) HTML elements
3. How do you retrieve stored data from an HTML element using **`.data()`**?
   a) Using `.getData('key')`
   b) Using `.data('key')`
   c) Using `.retrieveData('key')`
   d) Using `.fetch('key')`
4. What does the `.index()` method in jQuery allows you to determine?
   a) The HTML tag name of an element
   b) The index position of an element in relation to its siblings
   c) The total number of elements in the DOM
   d) The CSS class of an element

Answers

1. b) Attaching custom data to an HTML element
2. c) Strings, numbers, objects, or arrays
3. b) Using `.data('key')`
4. b) The index position of an element in relation to its siblings

CHAPTER 10

Handling Events with jQuery

Introduction

This chapter covers event handling with jQuery, an essential aspect of developing interactive web applications. The chapter starts with a brief overview of the event model in JavaScript and then dives into how to use jQuery to bind and trigger events. Readers will learn about the various event methods in jQuery, such as `.click()`, `.hover()`, `.submit()`, and `.keypress()`, and how to use them to handle user interactions with the page.

The chapter also covers more advanced event-handling techniques, such as using event delegation to handle events on dynamically created elements and using the `.on()` method to bind multiple events at once. Readers will also learn about event bubbling and propagation and how to use event methods like `.stopPropagation()` and `.preventDefault()` to control the behavior of events.

The chapter concludes with a discussion of best practices for event handling with jQuery, including how to optimize event handling for performance and how to organize event handlers for clarity and maintainability.

By the end of this chapter, readers will have a comprehensive understanding of how to handle events with jQuery and how to use the various event methods and techniques to create rich, interactive web applications.

- Mouse move listeners and hover events with jQuery
- Listening for keyboard events and getting values from the event object with jQuery
- Handling form events with jQuery
- Using the on method to attach events with more powerful events

Events play a crucial role in creating interactive and dynamic web applications. In this chapter, we will explore event handling with jQuery, an essential aspect of web development. We will start with a brief overview of the event model in JavaScript to provide a solid foundation for understanding how events work in web development.

Structure

In this chapter, we will cover the following topics:

- Overview of Event Handling in JavaScript
- Introduction to the concept of events in web development
- Explanation of how jQuery simplifies event handling
- Explanation of various event methods in jQuery, including **`.click()`**, **`.hover()`**, **`.submit()`**, and **`.keypress()`**
- Demonstrating how to use these methods to handle user interactions
- Event delegation: Handling events on dynamically created elements
- Using the **`.on()`** method to bind multiple events simultaneously
- Explanation of event bubbling and propagation in the DOM
- Introduction to event methods like **`.stopPropagation()`** and **`.preventDefault()`** for controlling event behavior
- Demonstrating how to listen for mouse move events and handle hover events using jQuery
- Listening for keyboard events
- Extracting values from the event object in jQuery
- Exploring how to handle events related to HTML forms using jQuery

Understanding Event Handling

The event model in JavaScript allows developers to respond to various interactions and activities on a web page. This can include actions like mouse clicks, keyboard inputs, form submissions, and more. However, working with raw JavaScript to handle events can be cumbersome and complex. This is where jQuery comes in as a powerful tool for simplifying event handling and making it more efficient.

jQuery Event Methods

jQuery provides a wide range of event methods that streamline the process of binding and triggering events. These methods are designed to simplify event handling, making it easier for developers to respond to user interactions effectively. Some of the commonly used event methods include:

.click()

The **.click()** method allows you to respond to mouse-click events on specific elements. This is often used to create interactive features like buttons and links.

```
<!DOCTYPE html>
<html>
<head>
  <title>Click Example</title>
  <script src="https://code.jquery.com/jquery-3.6.0.min.js"></script>
</head>
<body>

<button id="myButton">Click me</button>
<div id="output">Click the button to see the result.</div>

<script>
  // Wait for the document to be ready
  $(document).ready(function() {
    // Attach a click event handler to the button with the id "myButton"
    $('#myButton').click(function() {
      // This function will be executed when the button is clicked
      $('#output').text('Button clicked!');
    });
  });
</script>

</body>
</html>
```

1. We include the jQuery library in the **<head>** section of the HTML document.
2. We have a button with the id "**myButton**" and a **<div>** with the id "**output**" in the HTML body.
3. Inside the <script> section, we use **$(document).ready()** to ensure that the code is executed after the document is fully loaded.
4. We select the button with **$('#myButton')** and use the .**click()** method to attach a click event handler to it.
5. When the button is clicked, the provided function is executed, and it changes the text of the <div> with the id "**output**" to "**Button clicked**!"

This example demonstrates a simple use case of the **.click()** method to respond to a button click event using jQuery.

.hover()

The **.hover()** method enables you to respond to mouse hover events, which occur when the cursor enters and exits an element. This is useful for creating interactive tooltips and dropdown menus.

```
<!DOCTYPE html>
<html>
<head>
  <title>Hover Example</title>
  <script src="https://code.jquery.com/jquery-3.6.0.min.js"></script>
  <style>
    #myDiv {
      width: 200px;
      height: 100px;
      background-color: lightblue;
    }
  </style>
</head>
<body>

<div id="myDiv">Hover over me</div>
```

```
<div id="output">Mouse is not over the element.</div>


<script>
  // Wait for the document to be ready
  $(document).ready(function() {
    // Select the element with the id "myDiv" and use .hover() to attach hover event handlers
    $('#myDiv').hover(
      function() {
        // This function is executed when the mouse enters the element
        $('#output').text('Mouse entered the element.');
      },
      function() {
        // This function is executed when the mouse leaves the element
        $('#output').text('Mouse left the element.');
      }
    );
  });
</script>


</body>
</html>
```

1. We include the jQuery library in the **<head>** section of the HTML document.
2. We have **<div>** with the id "**myDiv**" and another <div> with the id "**output**" in the HTML body. The "**myDiv**" element is styled with CSS.
3. Inside the **<script>** section, we use **$(document).ready()** to ensure that the code is executed after the document is fully loaded.
4. We select the element with the id "**myDiv**" and use the **.hover()** method to attach both "**mouseenter**" and "**mouseleave**" event handlers. The first function is executed when the mouse enters the element, and the second function is executed when the mouse leaves the element.
5. When the mouse hovers over "**myDiv**," the "**Mouse entered the element**" text is displayed in the "**output**" div. When the mouse leaves the element, the text changes to "**Mouse left the element**."

This example demonstrates how to use the **.hover()** method in jQuery to respond to mouse hover events on an element and perform actions when the mouse enters or leaves the element.

.submit()

The **.submit()** method is used to handle form submission events. It allows you to validate form data and prevent the default form submission if necessary.

```
<!DOCTYPE html>
<html>
<head>
  <title>Submit Example</title>
  <script src="https://code.jquery.com/jquery-3.6.0.min.js"></script>
</head>
<body>

<form id="myForm">
  <label for="name">Name:</label>
  <input type="text" id="name" name="name" required>
  <br>
  <label for="email">Email:</label>
  <input type="email" id="email" name="email" required>
  <br>
  <input type="submit" value="Submit">
</form>

<div id="output"></div>

<script>
  // Wait for the document to be ready
  $(document).ready(function() {
    // Select the form with the id "myForm" and use .submit() to capture
the form submission event
    $('#myForm').submit(function(event) {
      // Prevent the default form submission
```

```
      event.preventDefault();

      // Get the values entered in the form fields
      const name = $('#name').val();
      const email = $('#email').val();

      // Display the form data in the "output" div
      $('#output').html(`Name: ${name}<br>Email: ${email}`);
    });
  });

</script>

</body>
</html>
```

1. We include the jQuery library in the **<head>** section of the HTML document.
2. We have a **<form>** element with the id "**myForm**" containing two input fields for name and email. There's also a submit button.
3. Inside the <**script**> section, we use **$(document).ready()** to ensure that the code is executed after the document is fully loaded.
4. We select the form with the id "**myForm**" and use the .**submit()** method to capture the form submission event. The provided function takes the event object as a parameter.
5. Within the event handler, we prevent the default form submission using **event.preventDefault()** to stop the page from reloading.
6. We retrieve the values entered in the name and email fields using **.val()**.
7. Finally, we display the form data in the "**output**" div.

When the user submits the form, the data entered in the form fields is captured, and their values are displayed in the "**output**" div without the page being reloaded. This demonstrates how to use the **.submit()** method in jQuery to capture form submission events and handle them as needed.

.keypress()

The **.keypress()** method is used to capture keyboard input events. You can use it to create features like search bars or keyboard shortcuts.

```
<!DOCTYPE html>
<html>
<head>
  <title>Keypress Example</title>
  <script src="https://code.jquery.com/jquery-3.6.0.min.js"></script>
</head>
<body>

<input type="text" id="myInput">
<p id="output">Key pressed: </p>

<script>
  // Wait for the document to be ready
  $(document).ready(function() {
    // Select the input field with the id "myInput" and use .keypress()
to capture keypress events
    $('#myInput').keypress(function(event) {
      // Get the key code of the pressed key
      const keyCode = event.which;

      // Display the key code in the "output" paragraph
      $('#output').text('Key pressed: ' + keyCode);
    });
  });
</script>

</body>

</html>
```

1. Include the jQuery library in the `<head>` section of the HTML document.
2. Have an `<input>` element with the id "`myInput`" where users can type text.
3. There's a `<p>` element with the id "`output`" to display information about the key pressed.
4. Inside the `<script>` section, we use `$(document).ready()` to ensure that the code is executed after the document is fully loaded.
5. Select the input field with the id "`myInput`" and use the `.keypress()` method to capture keypress events. The provided function takes the event object as a parameter.
6. Within the event handler, we use `event.which` to get the key code of the pressed key.
7. Then display the key code in the "`output`" paragraph.

When you type in the input field, the key codes of the pressed keys are captured, and their values are displayed in the "`output`" paragraph.

Mouse Events

In jQuery, mouse events allow developers to respond to user interactions with a web page through actions like clicking, hovering, moving, and dragging the mouse cursor, enabling the creation of an interactive and engaging user interface.

jQuery mouse events respond to user mouse interactions like clicks, hovers, drags, and releases. Easily attach listeners to HTML elements, executing custom code in response to various mouse actions.

`.hover()`

Function: This method is used to assign functions to be executed when the mouse pointer enters and leaves an element.

Explanation: In the code, all the `<div>` elements with the class "`box`" within the .main container have the `.hover()` method applied. When the mouse enters any of these divs, it changes their background color to red, and when the mouse leaves, it resets the background color to white.

.mouseup()

The `.mouseup()` method in jQuery is used to assign a function that will be executed when the mouse button is released (clicked and then released) while the pointer is positioned over an HTML element. It allows you to perform actions in response to the mouse button being released. For example, you can change the appearance or behavior of an element after the user releases a mouse button. It's commonly used for interactive features like buttons or elements that respond to clicks. This event can be used in conjunction with `.mousedown()` to create click-like functionality where you respond to both mouse button presses and releases.

Function: This method assigns a function to be executed when a mouse button is released over an element.

Explanation: In the code, when a mouse button is released over any of the `<div>` elements with the class "`box`," it changes their text content to "`MOUSE UP`" and the background color to blue.

.mousedown()

The `.mousedown()` method in jQuery is used to assign a function that will be executed when the mouse button is pressed down (clicked) while the pointer is positioned over an HTML element. It allows you to perform actions in response to the mouse button being pressed. For example, you can change the appearance or behavior of an element when the user clicks on it. It's commonly used for creating interactive features, such as button clicks or drag-and-drop functionality. This event is often used in conjunction with the `.mouseup()` event to create functionality that responds to both mouse button presses and releases.

Function: This method assigns a function to be executed when a mouse button is pressed down over an element.

Explanation: In the code, when a mouse button is pressed down over any of the `<div>` elements with the class "`box,`" it changes their text content to "`MOUSE DOWN`" and the background color to green.

.mouseout()

The `.mouseout()` method in jQuery is used to assign a function that will be executed when the mouse pointer moves out of an HTML element. It is triggered when the mouse exits the boundaries of the selected element. This event is useful for scenarios where you want to take action when the user moves their mouse away from a particular area or element, such as hiding a tooltip when the mouse is no longer over the tooltip-triggering element. It is the opposite of the `.mouseover()` event, which triggers when the mouse enters an element's boundaries.

Function: This method assigns a function to be executed when the mouse pointer leaves the element.

Explanation: When the mouse pointer leaves the .main container, the text content of the div with the class "`div2`" changes to "`Mouse OUT on MAIN!`"

.mouseover()

The `.mouseover()` method in jQuery is used to assign a function that will be executed when the mouse pointer moves over an HTML element. It is triggered when the mouse enters the boundaries of the selected element. This event is commonly used to create interactive effects when a user hovers their mouse over an element, such as showing tooltips or changing the appearance of an element. It is the opposite of the `.mouseout()` event, which triggers when the mouse leaves an element's boundaries.

Function: This method assigns a function to be executed when the mouse pointer enters the element.

Explanation: When the mouse pointer enters the .main container, the text content of the div with the class "`div2`" changes to "`Mouse OVER on MAIN!`"

.mouseleave()

The `.mouseleave()` method in jQuery is used to assign a function that will be executed when the mouse pointer leaves the boundaries of an HTML element. It is triggered when the mouse exits the area of the selected element. This event is commonly used to create interactive effects when a user moves their mouse out of an element, such as hiding tooltips or restoring the element's original appearance. It is the opposite of the `.mouseenter()` event, which triggers when the mouse enters an element's boundaries.

Function: This method assigns a function to be executed when the mouse pointer leaves the element.

Explanation: When the mouse pointer leaves the .main container, the text content of the div with the class "`div3`" changes to "`Mouse LEFT on MAIN!`"

.mouseenter()

The **.mouseenter()** method in jQuery is used to assign a function that will be executed when the mouse pointer enters the boundaries of an HTML element. It is triggered when the mouse hovers over the selected element. This event is commonly used to create interactive effects when a user moves their mouse into an element, such as displaying tooltips or changing the element's appearance. It is often paired with the **.mouseleave()** event to handle mouse entry and exit events for an element.

Function: This method assigns a function to be executed when the mouse pointer enters the element.

Explanation: When the mouse pointer enters the .main container, the text content of the div with the class "**div3**" changes to "**Mouse ENTER on MAIN!**"

.mousemove()

The **.mousemove()** method in jQuery is used to attach a function that will be executed whenever the mouse pointer moves over a selected HTML element. This event is triggered continuously as the mouse cursor is in motion within the element's boundaries. It is commonly used to track the mouse's position and create interactive features like updating coordinates or following the mouse's movement. The event handler receives information about the mouse's current position, which can be used for various purposes in web applications.

Function: This method assigns a function to be executed when the mouse pointer moves over the document.

Explanation: When the mouse pointer moves anywhere over the document, the text content of the div with the class "**div1**" changes to display the current X and Y coordinates of the mouse pointer.

jQuery mouse moves events listeners and hover events

Exercise: Attach various mouse movement events to page elements.

1. Add the **hover()** event to the divs within the main class. On entering, update the background color to red and then on leave set it back to white.
2. Add **mouseup()** and **mousedown()** to the divs updating the text and the color of the background on the different mouse press states.

3. Add **mouseout()** and **mouseleave()** to the main element, and check the difference.

4. Add **mouseenter()** and **mouseover()** to the main element, check the difference.

5. Add **mouseenter()** and **mouseleave()** to the buttons, to update the background color just like the **hover()** event.

6. On the main document track the **mousemove()** from the event object, get the values of **pageX** and **pageY** property values and then output them into a page element.

CSS Code:

```
.box{
border:1px solid #ddd;
height:50px;
width:100px;
}
```

HTML Code:

```
<nav>
<div class="main">
<div class="div1">Hello World 1</div>
<div class="div2"><span>Hello World 2</span></div> <div class="div3"
id="div3">Hello World 3</div>
<div class="div4">Laurence Svekis</div>

<button id="btn1">1</button>


<button id="btn2">2</button>
<button id="btn3">3</button>
<span class="span1">Hello</span>
</div>
</nav>
<button id="btn4">4</button>
<button id="btn5">5</button>
```

JavaScript Code:

```
$('.main div').addClass('box').hover(function(){ $(this).css('background
-color','red')},function(){ $(this).css('background-color','white')
}).mouseenter(function(e){
//$(this).text(`(X:${e.pageX} Y:${e.pageY}`);
})
$('.main div').mouseup(function(){
$(this).text('MOUSE UP');
$(this).css('background-color','blue');
}).mousedown(function(){
$(this).text('MOUSE DOWN');
$(this).css('background-color','green');


})
$('.main').mouseout(()=>{
$('.div2').text('Mouse OUT on MAIN!'); })
$('.main').mouseover(()=>{
$('.div2').text('Mouse OVER on MAIN!'); })
$('.main').mouseleave(()=>{
$('.div3').text('Mouse LEFT on MAIN!'); })
$('.main').mouseenter(()=>{
$('.div3').text('Mouse ENTER on MAIN!'); })
$('button').css('width','100px');
$('button').mouseenter(function(e){
$(this).css('background-color','red');
})
$('button').mouseleave(function(){
$(this).css('background-color','white'); })
$(document).mousemove(function(e){
$('.div1').text(`(X:${e.pageX} Y:${e.pageY}`); })
```

Overall, the provided code illustrates how various mouse-related events can be used to enhance interactivity in a web page, from changing element appearance to displaying information based on mouse interactions.

jQuery to listen for keyboard events and get values from the event object

CSS Code:

```
.box {
border: 1px solid #ddd;
height: 50px;
width: 100px;
}
input{
display:block;
}
```

HTML Code:

```
<div class="main"></div>
<button id="btn1">1</button>
<button id="btn2">2</button>
<button id="btn3">3</button>
```

JavaScript Code

Exercise Step 1: Using a loop, create several input fields and add them all to the main.

```
for (let i = 0; i < 10; i++) {
  const html = `Laurence ${i}`;
  adder(html);
}
```

Exercise Step 2: On the input field, add the **`keydown()`** method to update the CSS background color and output the event method into the console, including the element **`index()`** value.

```
$('input').keydown(function(e) {
  console.log(e.key, e.code);
  $(this).css('background-color', 'yellow');
  console.log('keydown ' + $(this).index());
})
```

Exercise Step 3: On the input field, add the **`keypress()`** method to update the CSS background color and output the keypress into the console, including the element **`index()`** value.

```
$('input').keypress(function(e) {
  console.log(e.key, e.code);
  $(this).css('background-color', 'red');
  console.log('keypress ' + $(this).index());
})
```

Exercise Step 4: On the input field, add **`focus()`** and **`blur()`** methods to update the CSS background color and output the event methods into the console, including the element **`index()`** value.

```
$('input').focus(function(e) {
  $(this).css('color', 'red');
  console.log('focus ' + $(this).index());
})

$('input').blur(function(e) {
  $(this).css('color', 'green');
  console.log('blur ' + $(this).index());
})
```

Exercise Step 5: On the input field, add the **`keyup()`** method to update the CSS background color and output the event method into the console, including the element **`index()`** value.

```
$('input').keyup(function(e) {
  console.log(e.key, e.code);
  $(this).css('background-color', 'white');
  console.log('keyup ' + $(this).index());
})
```

Exercise Step 6: On the input field, add **focusin()** and **focusout()** methods which will include the children, then update the CSS background color and output the event methods into the console, including the element **index()** value.

```
$('input').focusin(function(e) {
  $(this).css('color', 'blue');
  console.log('focusIn ' + $(this).index());
})

$('input').focusout(function(e) {
  $(this).css('color', 'pink');
  console.log('focusOut ' + $(this).index());
})

Function to Add Input Fields (adder):
function adder(val) {
  $('<input>').attr({
    type: 'text',
    value: val
  }).appendTo('.main');
}
```

This code accomplishes the tasks specified in each exercise step, including creating input fields, handling various events, updating CSS styles, and logging relevant information to the console.

This HTML code defines a simple web page with a div element having the class "**main**" and three buttons with IDs "**btn1**," "**btn2**," and "**btn3**."

The JavaScript code performs the following:

1. It uses a for loop to generate a series of input elements inside the **.main** div. Each input element is given a value like "**Laurence 0**," "**Laurence 1**," and so on. These input elements are created by calling the adder function.
2. Event handlers are attached to the input elements:
   a. The **.keydown()**, **.keypress()**, and **.keyup()** events are used to capture keyboard-related events. These events log information about the key pressed and change the background color of the corresponding input

element. The keydown, keypress, and keyup events are logged, along with the index of the input element in which the event occurred.

b. The **`.focus()`** and **`.blur()`** events are used to handle the input elements' focus and blur events. When an input element receives focus, its text color is changed to red, and when it loses focus, its text color is changed to green. The events are logged along with the input element's index.

c. The **`.focusin()`** and **`.focusout()`** events are similar to the **`.focus()`** and **`.blur()`** events but handle the input elements' **`focusin`** and **`focusout`** events instead. The text color is changed to blue when gaining focus and to pink when losing focus. These events are also logged with the input element's index.

In summary, this code generates a series of input elements and demonstrates how to handle keyboard-related events and focus and blur events using jQuery. The events trigger different visual Changes on the input elements and log relevant information to the console.

jQuery form Events on submit and more

Exercise: Attach events to form elements and form submission:

1. Add a select element with options to the HTML page.
2. On change of the select output the value to the element with the class of output.
3. Select the input text type element, and on change event output the value of the input field to the output element.
4. On the input field select of text, add a **`select()`** method event to the element, and output the active element text into the output element.
5. On the form submission, add an event which says in the console that the form was submitted, as well as add a **`preventDefault()`** to prevent the default action of form submission.
6. On a button add when clicked, add within the callback function that the main form is submitted.

CSS Code:

```
.box {
border: 1px solid #ddd;
height: 50px;
width: 100px;
}
input{
display:block;
}
```

HTML:

```
<div class="output"></div>
<form class="main">
<input type="text" name="name" value="Laurence Svekis"> <input type="-
submit" value="Submit">
</form>
<button id="btn1">1</button>
```

JavaScript:

```
$('<select>').appendTo('.main');
for(let i=0;i<5;i++){

const counter = `${i+1} Value`;
$('<option>').val(counter).text(counter).appendTo('select'); }
$('select').change(function(){
$('.output').text($(this).val());
})
$('input[type="text"]').change(function(){ $('.output').text($(this).
val());
})
$(':input').select(function(){
$('.output').text($(this).val());
})
$('.main').submit(function(e){
e.preventDefault();
```

```
console.log('form submitted');
})
$('#btn1').click(()=>{
$('.main').submit();
})
```

1. A **<select>** element with several **<option>** elements is added to the HTML page. The options are generated in a loop and appended to the select element.
2. A change event is attached to the **<select>** element. When the selected option in the dropdown changes, the value of the selected option is displayed in an element with the class "**output**." This allows the user to see the selected value.
3. The **<input>** element with the attribute **type="text"** is selected, and a change event is attached to it. When the text in the input field changes, the value of the input field is displayed in the "**output**" element.
4. All input elements (for example, text inputs) are selected using the **:input** selector, and a select event is attached to them. When an input field is selected (for example, by clicking into it), the value of the selected input field is displayed in the "**output**" element.
5. The **<form>** element with the class "**main**" is selected, and a submit event is attached to it. When the form is submitted, this event handler prevents the default form submission action using **e.preventDefault()**. It also logs a message to the console, indicating that the form has been submitted.
6. A button with the ID "**btn1**" is selected. When this button is clicked, a click event handler triggers the form submission by calling **$('.main').submit()**.

In summary, this code demonstrates how to use jQuery to handle events for various form elements and how to prevent the default form submission action. It also shows how to trigger the form submission programmatically when a button is clicked. The selected values from the form elements are displayed in the "**output**" element.

Conclusion

This chapter thoroughly explores event handling with jQuery, a crucial aspect of web development. Beginning with an overview of the JavaScript event model, jQuery's robust methods like `.click()`, `.hover()`, and `.submit()`, empower readers to adeptly manage user interactions. It provides an exploration of mouse events, ensuring a versatile toolkit for handling various mouse-related interactions, along with practical guidance on jQuery mouse move listeners and hover events. Additionally, the chapter covers listening for keyboard events and extracting values from the event object, enhancing developers' proficiency. Emphasizing the significance of jQuery form events, the chapter concludes by imparting insights into optimizing performance and organizational best practices, equipping readers to create dynamic and interactive web applications efficiently.

Coming up in the next chapter, on event delegation in jQuery introduces readers to the versatile `.on()` method. Emphasizing the efficiency of event delegation for dynamically created elements, the chapter explores event bubbling and propagation, demonstrating their roles in tailoring event behavior. A practical example with `.stopPropagation()` highlights effective event control. Additionally, the chapter extends its coverage to browser and window events, concluding with a hands-on exercise on jQuery scroll events, providing readers with a comprehensive toolkit for creating responsive and interactive web applications.

Chapter 11
Advanced Event Handling Techniques

Introduction

We'll focus on the efficient use of the `.on()` method for handling events. Engage in exercises to understand event attachment intricacies and enhance skills with more powerful interactions. The chapter covers key concepts like event bubbling and propagation, clarifying their roles in shaping event behavior. A practical example using `.stopPropagation()` helps master precise event control. The chapter concludes with hands-on exercises on jQuery scroll events, empowering readers to create responsive web applications effectively.

Structure

In this chapter, we will cover the following topics:

- Introduction to Event Delegation
- The Versatile `.on()` Method
- Event Bubbling and Propagation
- Example of `.stopPropagation()`
- Exercise on jQuery Scroll Events

Beyond the basic event methods, this chapter covers more advanced event-handling techniques.

Event delegation

Event delegation is a powerful approach for handling events on dynamically created elements. It allows you to attach event handlers to a parent element and capture events from its children, reducing the need for individual event bindings.

The .on() method

The **.on()** method is a versatile way to attach multiple events to elements. It simplifies event binding, making it easier to manage multiple interactions on a single element.

```
<button id="myButton">Click Me</button>


JavaScript (jQuery):
$(document).ready(function() {
  // Attach a click event handler to the button element with the ID
"myButton"
  $('#myButton').on('click', function() {
    alert('Button clicked!');
  });
});
```

In this example, when the document is ready (that is, the DOM is fully loaded), a click event handler is attached to the button element with the ID "**myButton**." When the button is clicked, it triggers the click event, and the event handler displays an alert with the message "**Button clicked!**"

The **.on()** method provides a way to handle various events, including click, hover, keypress, and more, and it's a powerful tool for event delegation and dynamic event handling in jQuery.

Exercise: Attach events with the on Method with more powerful events

Exercise: Use of **on()** method for adding events to future elements created after the event code is run.

1. Create an element with a class of boxes, and add it to the start at the top of the page elements.
2. Add multiple events to the element with a class of box, **`click()`**, **`mouseenter()`**, and **`mouseleave()`**.
3. Add to all the button elements within the **`.btns`** class element, the click event with the **`on()`** method. Once clicked, it should output the element index value to the text area of the element with the class of output.
4. Create an object with some data, then, using the **`on()`** method, add a click event, including the data to be sent to the callback function of the adder.
5. In the **`adder()`** function output the event object data into the console.
6. Use the shorthand click on the button elements, add when clicked that the background changes to red and the element index value is output into the console log. 7. Create page buttons and append them to the **`btns`** class element. The buttons created after the **`click()`** event was added will not have the click event.

CSS:

```
.box {
border: 1px solid #ddd;
height: 50px;
width: 100px;
}

input{
display:block;
}
.active{
background-color:red;
color:green;
}
```

HTML:

```
<div class="output"></div>
<div class="btns">
<button id="btn1">1</button>
```

```
<button id="btn2">2</button>
<button id="btn3">3</button>
</div>
```

JavaScript:

```
$('<div>').text('LaurenceSvekis').addClass('box').prependTo('bod y');
$('.box').on({

click : function() {$(this).toggleClass('active')}, mouseenter:func-
tion(){$(this).css('background-color','blue')} ,
mouseleave:function(){$(this).css('background-color','white')} })
$('.btns').on('click','button',function(){
const val = `${$(this).index()} index button`;
$('.output').text(val);
})
const obj = {
first : 'Laurence',
last : 'Svekis',
id : 100
};
$('.output').on('click',obj,adder);
function adder(e){
console.log(e.data);
}
$('.btns button').click(function(){
const val = `${$(this).index()} index button`;
$(this).css('background-color','red');
console.log(val);
})

for(let i=0;i<5;i++){
const temp = `${i+4}`;
$('<button>').text(temp).appendTo('.btns');
}
```

The HTML document contains a div element with the class "**`output`**" and another div with the class "**`btns`**" containing three buttons.

1. A div element with the class "**`box`**" is dynamically created, styled, and added to the body.
2. Event handling is attached to the "**`box`**" elements using the **`.on()`** method. Three events (**`click`**, **`mouseenter`**, and **`mouseleave`**) are defined. When you click a "**`box`**," it toggles the "**`active`**" class, changing the background color and text color. Mouse enter and leave events to change the background color.
3. Event delegation is used to handle button clicks within the "**`btns`**" div. When a button is clicked, its index and a message are displayed in the "**`output`**" div.
4. A custom data object (**`obj`**) is associated with the "**`output`**" div to be used in click events. When you click the "**`output`**" div, the data is logged to the console.
5. Additional event handling for the dynamically created buttons in the "**`btns`**" div. When you click these buttons, the index and a background color change are displayed.
6. A loop creates and appends five buttons to the "**`btns`**" div.

This code demonstrates the use of event handling, event delegation, dynamic event handling, and custom data in jQuery.

Understanding Event Bubbling and Propagation

Events in the Document Object Model (DOM) can propagate in different ways, affecting how they are handled. Understanding event bubbling and propagation is crucial for controlling event behavior. How events propagate through the DOM and how to use event methods like **`.stopPropagation()`** and **`.preventDefault()`** to control and modify this behavior.

Example of `.stopPropagation()`:

The **`.stopPropagation()`** method is used to prevent the event from propagating to parent elements. It stops the event from "**`bubbling up`**" the DOM tree.

```
<div id="parent">
  <button id="child">Click Me</button>
</div>
<script>
  $(document).ready(function() {
    $("#child").click(function(event) {
      alert("Child button clicked!");
      event.stopPropagation(); // Prevent the event from reaching the
parent
    });

    $("#parent").click(function() {
      alert("Parent div clicked!");
    });
  });
</script>
```

In this example, when you click the "**`Click Me`**" button, it triggers an alert, and the **`.stopPropagation()`** method prevents the click event from propagating to the parent div. So, you will only see the "**`Child button clicked!`**" alert. If you remove the **`.stopPropagation()`** you will see the second alert after the first one is closed.

Example of `.preventDefault()`:

The **`.preventDefault()`** method is used to prevent the default behavior of certain HTML elements, such as links and form submissions.

```
<a id="link" href="https://www.example.com">Click Me</a>
<form id="myForm">
  <input type="text" name="username" placeholder="Enter your username">
  <button type="submit">Submit</button>
</form>
<script>
  $(document).ready(function() {
    $("#link").click(function(event) {
      event.preventDefault(); // Prevent the link from navigating to
another page
```

```
      alert("Link clicked, but default behavior prevented.");
    });

    $("#myForm").submit(function(event) {
      event.preventDefault(); // Prevent the form from submitting
      alert("Form submitted, but default behavior prevented.");
    });
  });
</script>
```

In this example, when you click the "**`Click Me`**" link or submit the form, the **`.preventDefault()`** method is used to prevent the default behavior (navigating to another page or submitting the form). Instead, an alert message is displayed.

These examples illustrate how to use **`.stopPropagation()`** and **`.preventDefault()`** to control event propagation and default behaviors in your web applications using jQuery.

Exercise: jQuery scroll event on Browser Events and Window events

Figure 11.1 shows image of links that can be clicked to scroll the page automatically:

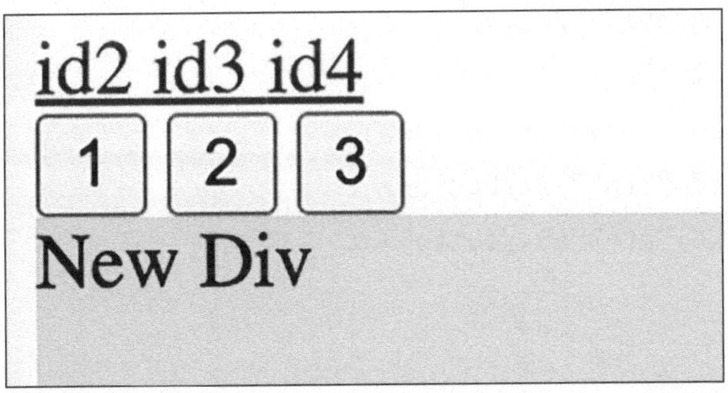

Figure 11.1: *Image of links that can be clicked to scroll the page automatically*

Exercise: Add elements and connect the anchor tag to the elements with id, add an event of the scroll and resize to the Window object.

1. When the button is clicked, create a random value to be used for height, and a random color to be used for the background color of a new element. Create a new **`div`**, set the **`css()`**, add an attribute of id and append it to the body of the page.

2. Add an anchor tag, with a hyperlink to the **#** + element id and append this to the element with a class of output.
3. Add a **scroll()** event to the window and a **resize()** to the window. Output those events to the console.

CSS Code:

```
.box {
    border: 1px solid #ddd;
    height: 50px;
    width: 100px;
}
input{
    display:block;
}
.active{
    background-color:red;
    color:green;
}
```

HTML Code:

```
<div class="output"></div>
<div class="btns">
    <button id="btn1">1</button>
    <button id="btn2">2</button>
    <button id="btn3">3</button>
</div>
```

JavaScript Code:

```
let counter = 1;
$('button').click(()=>{
   counter++;
   const r = Math.floor(Math.random()*200)+100;
   const c = '#'+Math.random().toString(16).substring(2,8);
   const id = 'id'+counter;
   $('<div>').text('New Div').css('height',r+'px').attr('id',id).
```

```
css('background-color',c).appendTo('body');
    //output
    $('<a>').attr('href','#'+id).text(id+' ').appendTo('.output');
})
$(window).scroll((e)=>{
    console.log(e);
})
$(window).resize((e)=>{
    console.log($(window).height());
    console.log($(document).height());
})
```

1. In the HTML the page has three buttons inside a div with the class "**btns**," and there's an empty div with the class "**output**."
2. In the JavaScript section, a counter variable is initialized to 1. It tracks the number of times a button is clicked.
3. An event handler is set up to respond to button clicks. When a button is clicked, the following actions occur:
    a. The counter is incremented.
    b. A random height (between 100 and 300 pixels) and a random background color are generated.
    c. An ID for a new **<div>** element is created using the increment counter.
    d. A new **<div>** element is created, with the text '**New Div**,' a specified height, a unique ID, and the generated background color.
    e. The new **<div>** element is appended to the body of the page.
    f. A new **<a>** element is created with an **href** attribute pointing to the newly created **<div>**'s ID. This link is added to the "**output**" div, creating a list of links to the generated **<div>** elements.
4. Additional event handlers are set up using jQuery:
    a. **$(window).scroll()**: When the user scrolls the page, this event handler logs information about the scroll event to the console.
    b. **$(window).resize()**: When the browser window is resized, this event handler logs the height of the window and the height of the document to the console.

In summary, the code dynamically generates and adds new colored `<div>` elements to the web page with unique IDs every time a button is clicked. It also creates a list of links to these generated `<div>` elements. Additionally, it provides event handlers to log information when the user scrolls or resizes the browser window.

Conclusion

This chapter provided a comprehensive overview of event handling in web development using the jQuery library. It covered various aspects of event management, starting with an introduction to the JavaScript event model and then delving into how jQuery can be utilized to bind and trigger events. The chapter discusses different jQuery event methods like `.click()`, `.hover()`, `.submit()`, and `.keypress()` for handling user interactions. Additionally, it explores more advanced event-handling techniques, including event delegation for dynamically created elements and the use of the `.on()` method to bind multiple events simultaneously. Readers will also learn about event bubbling, propagation control using methods like `.stopPropagation()` and `.preventDefault()`, and best practices for optimizing event handling and maintaining clear, organized event handlers. The chapter equips readers with the knowledge and skills to effectively manage events in web applications using jQuery. The chapter content also provides practical examples, such as handling mouse move listeners, hover events, keyboard events, and form events with jQuery, and demonstrates the power of the `.on()` method for attaching more powerful events.

The upcoming chapter focuses on the significant role of AJAX (Asynchronous JavaScript and XML) in creating highly responsive web applications, emphasizing the elimination of the need for page refreshes when handling user interactions. It initiates with an introduction to jQuery's essential AJAX capabilities, primarily the `$.ajax()` method, which equips readers with the ability to initiate HTTP requests and effectively manage server responses. The chapter further explores the customization of AJAX requests through options like type, URL, data, and dataType, tailoring them to specific application requirements.

In addition, readers will discover the convenience of jQuery's shorthand methods, including `$.get()`, `$.post()`, `$.getJSON()`, and `$.getScript`, designed to streamline the process of making AJAX requests while improving code clarity and readability. As the chapter progresses, it delves into the realm of callback options within jQuery, allowing developers to define functions that execute upon the completion of AJAX requests. These callback functions, such as success, error, and complete are examined to illustrate how they can effectively manage AJAX responses and errors.

Multiple Choice Questions

1. Which method in jQuery can be used to handle user interactions, such as clicking and hovering?

   a) `.bind()`

   b) `.eventHandler()`

   c) `.interact()`

   d) `.click()`

2. What is the purpose of using the .on() method in jQuery for event handling?

   a) To disable all event handling for an element

   b) To trigger an event programmatically

   c) To bind multiple events at once

   d) To prevent event propagation

3. Which jQuery method can be used to stop the propagation of an event to its parent elements?

   a) `.halt()`

   b) `.stopEvent()`

   c) `.stopPropagation()`

   d) `.preventDefault()`

4. How can the `.preventDefault()` method in jQuery be useful in event handling?

   a) It cancels the event execution completely.

   b) It prevents event bubbling.

   c) It triggers the event automatically.

   d) It enhances event delegation.

5. In jQuery, what method can be used to bind events to elements that match a specific selector, including dynamically created elements?

    a) `.register()`

    b) `.bind()`

    c) `.attach()`

    d) `.on()`

Answers

1. d) `.click()`
2. c) To bind multiple events at once
3. c) `.stopEvent()`
4. a) It cancels the event execution completely.
5. d) `.on()`

Chapter 12

jQuery AJAX Methods and Callback Options

Introduction

This chapter covers AJAX methods and callback options in jQuery. AJAX stands for Asynchronous JavaScript and XML and is a technique used to update a web page without refreshing it. With AJAX, web developers can create highly interactive applications that respond quickly to user input.

The chapter starts by introducing the **`$.ajax()`** method, which is the core of jQuery's AJAX functionality. Use this method to make HTTP requests and handle responses from a server. Different options can be passed to the **`$.ajax()`** methods, such as type, url, data, and dataType, and how to use them to customize AJAX requests.

Shorthand methods are available in jQuery for making AJAX requests, such as **`$.get()`**, **`$.post()`**, **`$.getJSON()`**, and **`$.getScript()`**. Learn how to use these shorthand methods to simplify AJAX requests and make code more readable.

The chapter concludes with a discussion of callback options in jQuery, which allow developers to define functions that will be executed when AJAX requests are complete. Readers will learn about the different callback functions available in jQuery, such as success, error, and complete, and how to use them to handle AJAX responses and errors.

By the end of this chapter, readers will have a comprehensive understanding of how to use AJAX methods and callback options in jQuery to create highly interactive and responsive web applications.

Structure

In this chapter, we will cover the following topics:

- Explanation of AJAX (Asynchronous JavaScript and XML) and its role in updating web pages without refreshing
- Introduction to the core jQuery method for making HTTP requests and handling responses
- Customizing AJAX requests using options like type, url, data, and dataType
- Overview of shorthand methods in jQuery for making common AJAX requests
- Demonstrations of **`$.get()`**, **`$.post()`**, **`$.getJSON()`**, and **`$.getScript()`** methods
- How to use the load method in jQuery to load content from external files into HTML elements
- Explanation of how to use **`$.get()`** to retrieve JSON data from a server and process it in jQuery
- How to use shorthand methods like **`$.getScript()`** and **`$.getJSON()`** for GET requests to load scripts and JSON data
- Introduction to callback options in jQuery, including success, error, and complete callbacks
- How to define functions to handle AJAX responses and errors

Introduction to AJAX with jQuery

`load()` method

The **`load()`** method in jQuery is a simple and convenient way to perform an AJAX request and load data from a server into a specific HTML element on a web page. It simplifies the process of fetching content from a server and updating the content of a designated element in your HTML. Here's an explanation of how the **`load()`** method works:

Basic Syntax:

```
$(selector).load(url, [data], [complete]);
```

1. `selector`: This is the HTML element where you want to load the content from the server.
2. `url`: The URL of the server-side resource (for example, an HTML file, a text file, or a specific server endpoint) that you want to fetch data from.
3. `data` (optional): An optional parameter that allows you to send data to the server, typically used with HTTP POST requests.
4. `complete` (optional): A callback function that is executed once the request is complete, which can be used for additional processing.

Exercise: AJAX example connects to an external file and loads the contents directly into a page element

Figure 12.1 shows exercise output with three clickable buttons (an example of the expected output from the exercise):

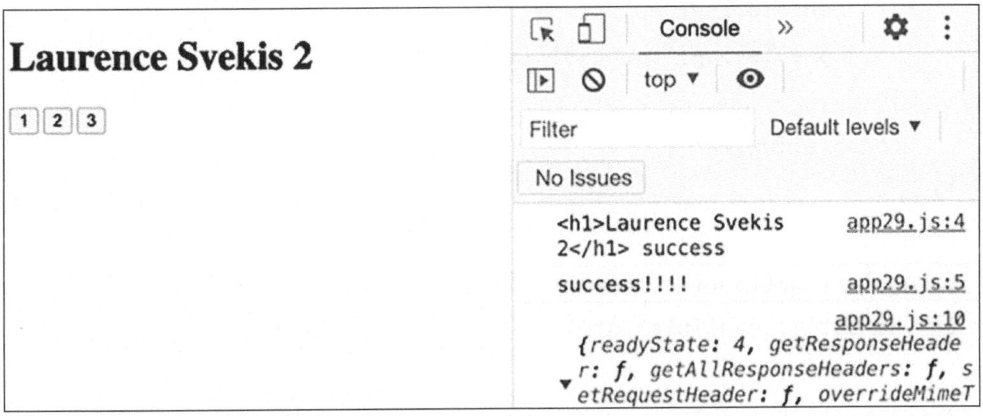

Figure 12.1: *Exercise output with 3 clickable buttons: this is an example of the expected output from the exercise*

1. Create several text and html files with content that you want to load directly into your page elements.
2. Using a click event on the button, and the **`load()`** method, select the element and in the load parameters add a string value of the path to the file.

3. An optional callback function can return the response text, the response status and the entire xHR object, which can then be used within the callback function. Check the status. If the status returns '**success**' then load a message into the console.

HTML

```
<div class="output"></div>
<div class="btns">
    <button id="btn1">1</button>
    <button id="btn2">2</button>
    <button id="btn3">3</button>
</div>
```

JavaScript

```
$('#btn1').click(()=>{
   $('.output').load('file1.txt',(rep,status,xhr)=>{
       if(status == 'success'){
           console.log(rep,status);
           console.log('success!!!!');
       }
       console.log(xhr);
   });
})
$('#btn2').click(()=>{
   $('.output').load('file1.html');
})
$('#btn3').click(()=>{
   $('.output').load('file1.txt');
})
```

The **$.ajax()** method forms the bedrock for making HTTP requests and handling server responses. Through key parameters like type, url, data, and dataType, developers can customize their AJAX interactions, unlocking the potential for a wide range of applications. The **$.ajax()** method in jQuery is a powerful and versatile function used to make asynchronous HTTP requests to a web server. It allows you to retrieve data from a server, send data to a server, or perform other actions without the need to reload the entire web page.

- **URL (Uniform Resource Locator)**: You specify the URL of the server-side resource you want to interact with. This can be a web page, an API endpoint, or any other resource that can handle HTTP requests.
- **HTTP Method (type)**: You can specify the HTTP method, such as GET, POST, PUT, DELETE, and so on, to indicate the type of request you want to make. GET is used for retrieving data, while POST is typically used for sending data to the server.
- **Data**: You can include data to send to the server, typically in the form of an object or a string. This is often used for sending form data or other information to the server.
- **DataType**: You specify the expected data type of the response from the server, such as JSON, XML, HTML, or text. jQuery will automatically parse the response based on this setting.
- **Success and Error Handlers**: You can define functions that will be executed when the request is successful (using the success parameter) or when there is an error (using the error parameter). These functions allow you to handle the response from the server appropriately.
- **Complete Handler**: You can also define a function to be executed when the request is completed, regardless of whether it was successful or not (using the complete parameter).
- **Other Settings**: `$.ajax()` provides many other settings and options for customizing your request, such as setting headers, handling timeouts, and enabling cross-origin requests.

Overall, `$.ajax()` is a versatile tool for handling various types of AJAX requests in web development, making it possible to interact with remote servers and retrieve or send data dynamically without reloading the entire web page.

In the `$.ajax()` method in jQuery, the `fail()` method allows you to specify a function that will be executed when the AJAX request encounters an error, providing a way to handle and respond to failed requests. On the other hand, the `always()` method allows you to define a function that will be executed regardless of whether the AJAX request succeeds or fails, making it useful for performing cleanup or finalization tasks after the request is complete.

Exercise: jQuery AJAX method and callback options

Use the `ajax()` method to connect to endpoints and use the response data within the web page elements.

1. Use the **ajax()** method, within the argument object add a property value for the url of the source file. Add a callback function for the successful property value. With the successful request, output the data values into the web page element.
2. Use the **ajax()** method and a GET method type, in the ajax argument object, set the url to the endpoint URL, set the type to GET, set the data to an object of the input field values and names, set the response data as dataType json.
3. Add chained methods to **ajax()** of **done()** which will fire the callback function once the connection has been successful. Use the data values returned from the server endpoint and add them to your web page elements.
4. Chain to the **ajax()** method, the **fail()** and **always()** methods and output the response data into the console.
5. Use the same code as the GET request and update the type to POST. This will now send the request as a POST with the data from the web page input elements.

User.json file:

```
{
   "firstName": "Laurence",
   "lastName": "Svekis",
   "para": {
      "first": "Laurence",
      "last": "Svekis"
   }
}


const url = 'https://script.google.com/macros/s/AKfycbzuGPGSdXCOOD9jQq4S
0sx-OQxlOdL70sC_Z4AmWsRC6jnaxnwg8HGWfMBvalb-aD4U/exec';
$('<input>').attr({
   type:'text',
   value:'Laurence',
   name:'first'
}).appendTo('.ins').before('First:').after('<br>');
```

```
$('<input>').attr({
   type:'text',
   value:'Svekis',
   name:'last'
}).appendTo('.ins').before('Last:').after('<br>');

$('#btn1').text('JSON File').click(()=>{
    $.ajax({
         url : 'user.json',
         success: (result)=>{
            console.log(result);
            const html = `AJAX with file JSON data ${result.firstName}
${result.lastName}`;
            $('<div>').html(html).appendTo('.output');
         }
    });
});

$('#btn2').text('AJAX GET').click(()=>{
   $.ajax({
        url:url,
        type:'GET',
        data:{
            first : $('input').first().val(),
            last : $('input').last().val()
        },
        dataType:'json'
   })
   .done((data)=>{
        console.log(data);
        const html = `AJAX with Data ${data.para.first} ${data.para.last}`;
        $('<div>').html(html).appendTo('.output');
   })
```

```
    .fail((err)=>{
        console.log(err);
    })
    .always((data)=>{
        console.log(data);
    })
})

$('#btn3').text('AJAX POST').click(()=>{
    $.ajax({
        url:url,
        type:'POST',
        data:{
            first : $('input').first().val(),
            last : $('input').last().val()
        },
        dataType:'json'
    })
    .done((data)=>{
        console.log(data);
        const html = `AJAX POST data ${data.para.first} ${data.para.last}`;
        $('<div>').html(html).appendTo('.output');
    })
    .fail((err)=>{
        console.log(err);
    })
    .always((data)=>{
        console.log(data);
    })
})
```

Streamlined AJAX with Shorthand Methods

jQuery's shorthand methods include **`$.get()`**, **`$.post()`**, **`$.getJSON()`**, and **`$.getScript()`**. These concise and easy-to-use methods simplify the process of making AJAX requests, enhancing code readability and maintainability.

`$.get( url [, data ] [, success ] [, dataType ] ):`

Explanation: The **`$.get()`** method is used to make an AJAX GET request to retrieve data from a server.

```
$.get("https://jsonplaceholder.typicode.com/posts/1", function(data) {
    console.log(data); // Display the retrieved data
});
```

`$.post( url [, data ] [, success ] [, dataType ] ):`

Explanation: The **`$.post()`** method is used to make an AJAX POST request to send data to a server.

```
$.post("https://jsonplaceholder.typicode.com/posts", { title: "New
Post", body: "This is the post body" }, function(data) {
    console.log(data); // Display the response from the server
});
```

`$.getJSON( url [, data ] [, success ] ):`

Explanation: The **`$.getJSON()`** method is used to make an AJAX GET request specifically for JSON data. It automatically parses the JSON response.

```
$.getJSON("https://jsonplaceholder.typicode.com/posts/1", function(data) {
    console.log(data); // Display the parsed JSON data
});
```

```
$.getScript( url [, success ] )
```

Explanation: The **`$.getScript()`** method is used to dynamically load and execute a JavaScript script from a server.

```
$.getScript("https://example.com/script.js", function() {
    // The external script has been loaded and executed
    // You can now use functions or variables defined in the loaded
script
});
```

These shorthand methods simplify the process of making common types of AJAX requests in jQuery. They provide a convenient way to perform GET and POST requests, retrieve JSON data, and load external scripts, reducing the amount of code you need to write for these common operations.

Callback Options for Handling AJAX Responses

One of the essential aspects of AJAX is managing the response from the server. These powerful tools enable developers to define functions that execute when AJAX requests are completed. Readers will discover various callback functions, such as success, error, and complete, which play a pivotal role in handling AJAX responses and errors.

Callback options in jQuery are functions that you can define to be executed when an AJAX request completes, providing a way to handle various aspects of the response from the server. Callbacks are an essential part of managing AJAX responses and errors effectively. Here's an explanation of the commonly used callback options for handling AJAX responses.

- **`success`:**

Explanation: The success callback is executed when the AJAX request is successful. It is typically used to handle the data received from the server.

```
$.ajax({
    url: "https://api.example.com/data",
    success: function(data) {
        // Handle the data from the server
```

```
        console.log(data);
    }
});
```

- **error**:

Explanation: The error callback is executed when there is an error with the AJAX request, such as a network issue or a server error. It is used to handle error conditions.

```
$.ajax({
    url: "https://api.example.com/data",
    error: function(xhr, status, error) {
        // Handle the error
        console.log("AJAX request failed with status: " + status);
    }
});
```

- **complete**:

Explanation: The complete callback is executed regardless of whether the request is successful or results in an error. It is often used to perform cleanup tasks or other actions after the request.

```
$.ajax({
    url: "https://api.example.com/data",
    complete: function() {
        // This code will run after the request is completed
        console.log("Request completed.");
    }
});
```

These callback options allow you to handle the various outcomes of an AJAX request effectively. You can use them to display data, manage errors, and perform actions after the request, ensuring your web application responds gracefully to different scenarios. Callbacks are a key feature of jQuery's AJAX functionality, providing flexibility and control over asynchronous interactions with web servers.

Get JSON data with jQuery get method

Endpoints you can use to make GET method requests with practice data: https://www.discoveryvip.com/shared/.

Exercise: Make and AJAX request to a JSON file and retrieve the values as an object in the code:

1. Create a JSON file locally and use the **`get()`** method to get the JSON object data.
2. Use the JSON object data by outputting the values into the web page once the button is clicked.
3. Make several different connections, create elements with jQuery and add the JSON response data values into the page elements.
4. Practice connecting with different objects. Try the endpoint URL in the browser to check to see if GET will work to retrieve the data.

HTML Code

```
<div class="output"></div>
<div class="btns">
    <button id="btn1">1</button>
    <button id="btn2">2</button>
    <button id="btn3">3</button>
</div>
```

JavaScript Code

```
$('#btn1').click(adder1);
$('#btn2').click(adder2);
$('#btn3').click(adder3);

function adder2(){
   $.get('https://www.discoveryvip.com/shared/people.json',(data)=>{
       console.log(data);
       $.each(data.people,(ind,val)=>{
           console.log(val.first);
```

```
        });
    })
}
function adder3(){
    $.get('books.json',(data)=>{
        console.log(data.books);
        let val1 = JSON.stringify(data.books);
        $.each(data.books,(ind,val)=>{
            val1 += `<div>(${val.title}) `;
            val1 += `(${val.author})</div>`;
        });
        $('<div>').html(val1).appendTo('.output');
    })
}

function adder1(){
    $.get('file1.json',(res)=>{
        console.log(res);
        let html = `${res.firstName} ${res.lastName}`;
        $('<h2>').text(html).appendTo('.output');
        const a = res.address;
        const val1 =
`${a.city}<br>${a.postalCode}<br>${a.state}<br>${a.streetAddress}`;
        $('<div>').html(val1).appendTo('.output');
        $ul = $('<ul>');
        $ul.appendTo('.output');
        $.each(res.phoneNumbers,(ind,val)=>{
            console.log(val);
            const temp = `${ind+1}. ${val.number} (${val.type})`;
            $('<li>').text(temp).appendTo($ul);
        })

    })
```

```
}
```

JSON

file1.json


```
{"firstName":"Laurence","lastName":"Svekis","isAlive":true,"age":25,"
address":{"streetAddress":"33 Street","city":"New
York","state":"NY","postalCode":"10044"},"phoneNumbers":[{"type":"home",
"number":"1222-1234"},{"type":"office","number":"333 567-1234"},{"type":
"mobile","number":"123 444-1234"}]}
```


books.json


```
{
 "books": [
 {
 "title": "Learn to Code",
 "author": "John Smith",
 "isbn": "324-23243"
 },
 {
 "title": "The Adventures JSON",
 "author": "Jason Jones",
 "isbn": "3324-2-444"
 },
 {
 "title": "New Objects",
 "author": "Jane Doe",
 "isbn": "2343-234-2433"
 }
 ]
}
```


people.json


```
{
  "people": [
```

```
    {
      "first": "Laurence"
      , "last": "Svekis"
    }
    , {
      "first": "Laurence"
      , "last": "Svekis"
    }
    , {
      "first": "Laurence"
      , "last": "Svekis"
    }
    , {
      "first": "Laurence"
      , "last": "Svekis"
    }
  ]
}
```

GET shorthand Methods jQuery `getScript` and `getJSON` methods

Exercise: jQuery offers several GET methods to either send GET data, import a JS file to use in the current file and return response data as JSON.

1. Create input elements for the page using jQuery.
2. On the first button click, make a get method request to the endpoint and retrieve the JSON data. Output the JSON data object contents to the web page. `get()` method.
3. On the second button click import a JavaScript JS script file. Include a function in the new JS file that can then be invoked. `getScript()` method.
4. Add a new button to the page that will invoke the new JS function when clicked, outputting the contents of the input field into the browser console.

5. On the third button click, get the endpoint data as JSON using the **getJSON()** method. The output part of the response object data, selecting it by the property value of the object into the console of the browser.

```
const url = 'https://script.google.com/macros/s/AKfycbzuGPGSdXCOOD9jQq4S0sx-OQxlOdL70sC_Z4AmWsRC6jnaxnwg8HGWfMBvalb-aD4U/exec';
$('<input>').attr({
   type:'text',
   value:'Laurence',
   name:'first'
}).appendTo('.ins').before('First:').after('<br>');
$('<input>').attr({
   type:'text',
   value:'Svekis',
   name:'last'
}).appendTo('.ins').before('Last:').after('<br>');
$('#btn1').click(adder1);
$('#btn2').click(adder2);
$('#btn3').click(adder3);
$('#btn1').text('GET with para');
$('#btn2').text('GET Script JS');
$('#btn3').text('GET JSON');
function adder1(){
   const obj1 = {
       first : $('input').first().val(),
       last : $('input').last().val()
   }
   $.get(url,obj1,call1);
}

function call1(rep){
   console.log(rep.para);
   $.each(rep.para,(prop,val)=>{
       console.log(val);
```

```
        const html = `${prop}[${val}]`;
        $('<div>').html(html).appendTo('.output');
    })
}

function adder2(){
    $.getScript('jsTwo.js',()=>{
        logger('test working!');
        $('<button>').text('Send Message').click(()=>{
            logger($('input').first().val());
        }).appendTo('.btns');
    })
}

function adder3(){
    const url1 = `${url}?id=5000`;
    $.getJSON(url1,(data)=>{
        console.log(data.para.id);
    })
}

JSTwo.js
function logger(val){
    console.warn(val);
}
```

Conclusion

This chapter equips readers with a comprehensive understanding of how to harness AJAX methods and leverage callback options in jQuery. By mastering these techniques, developers can create web applications that are highly interactive and exceptionally responsive to user interactions. Using the jQuery load method to load files, retrieving JSON data with the jQuery get method, and posting data with the post method provide real-world insights into the power and flexibility of jQuery's AJAX capabilities.

Multiple Choice Questions

1. What does AJAX stand for in the context of web development?
   a) Advanced JavaScript and XML
   b) Asynchronous JavaScript and XML
   c) Automated JavaScript and XHTML
   d) Active JavaScript and JSON
2. In jQuery's **`$.ajax()`** method, what can be customized using options like type, url, data, and dataType?
   a) The server's response time
   b) The client's browser version
   c) The AJAX request itself
   d) The user's IP address
3. Which jQuery shorthand method is commonly used for making an AJAX GET request to retrieve JSON data?
   a) `$.send()`
   b) `$.fetch()`
   c) `$.getJSON()`
   d) `$.request()`
4. When using **`$.post()`** in jQuery, what type of request is being made to the server?
   a) GET request
   b) POST request
   c) PUT request
   d) DELETE request
5. What is the purpose of the "success" callback function in an AJAX request?
   a) To handle errors in the response
   b) To perform actions after the request is complete

c) To send data to the server

d) To handle the successful response from the server

6. What is the main advantage of using shorthand methods like **`$.get()`** and **`$.post()`** in jQuery AJAX?

   a) They can handle any type of request

   b) They are more secure

   c) They simplify the code and make it more readable

   d) They provide better server performance

Answers

1. b) Asynchronous JavaScript and XML
2. c) The AJAX request itself
3. c) `$.getJSON()`
4. b) POST request
5. d) To handle the successful response from the server
6. c) They simplify the code and make it more readable

Conclusion

As you reflect on the extensive exploration of jQuery, you've gained a profound understanding of its capabilities in web development. Beginning with the foundational concepts of integrating jQuery into HTML files, selecting page and DOM elements using various selectors, and leveraging advanced selection techniques, you've established a solid knowledge base.

The journey progresses into the dynamic manipulation of web pages, where you've honed skills in controlling element visibility and creating seamless transitions using methods like `.hide()`, `.show()`, `.toggle()`, and various animation techniques. Further, you've delved into the manipulation of element contents, inserting new elements into web pages, and mastering DOM manipulation, including the addition and removal of classes, dynamic creation, and modification of elements.

To solidify your understanding, the book provides practical projects, inviting you to create a jQuery Dynamic List Project. These hands-on experiences allow you to apply jQuery concepts to real-world scenarios, reinforcing your skills and deepening your practical understanding.

The exploration extends to the manipulation of CSS properties and element attributes, empowering you to modify the appearance of page elements dynamically. Advanced techniques in traversing and selecting page elements take center stage, offering insights into navigating the DOM tree, selecting specific elements based on relationships, and employing advanced filtering techniques.

Key methods, such as jQuery `data()` and `index()`, are thoroughly explored, providing you with tools for efficient element manipulation. You've gained insights into handling events with jQuery, from basic methods like `.click()`

to advanced techniques such as event delegation and using `.on()` for binding multiple events simultaneously. Best practices for optimizing event handling performance and maintaining code clarity have been emphasized.

The exploration concludes with a comprehensive examination of jQuery AJAX methods and callback options. You've learned to make HTTP requests, handle responses from servers, and customize AJAX requests. Shorthand methods like `$.get()` and `$.post()` simplify AJAX requests, and callback options such as success and error provide strategies for handling AJAX responses and errors effectively.

As you wrap up this journey, consider leveraging the projects and code examples covered in the book to practice and deepen your understanding of jQuery. Apply the concepts learned to real-world scenarios, creating dynamic, interactive, and visually appealing web applications. This comprehensive understanding of jQuery equips you with a robust toolkit for effective web development, empowering you to innovate and create engaging online experiences.

Multiple Choice Questions

1. What is the purpose of the jQuery library?

   a) Graphic design

   b) Animation creation

   c) Web development

   d) Database management

2. Which method is used in jQuery to control the visibility of elements on a web page?

   a) `.toggle()`

   b) `.fadeIn()`

   c) `.slideUp()`

   d) `.append()`

3. In jQuery, what method is used to create smooth, gradual transitions between visible and hidden states?

   a) `.fadeToggle()`

   b) `.slideDown()`

c) `.append()`

d) `.after()`

4. Which jQuery method is used for inserting elements before or after an existing element?

   a) `.prepend()`

   b) `.after()`

   c) `.wrap()`

   d) `.append()`

5. What does the jQuery `.addClass()` method do?

   a) Removes a class from an element

   b) Adds a class to an element

   c) Modifies the text content of an element

   d) Slides an element up

6. Which jQuery method is used to navigate the DOM tree and select descendant elements of a selected element?

   a) `.closest()`

   b) `.next()`

   c) `.find()`

   d) `.prev()`

7. What is the purpose of the jQuery `data()` method?

   a) Styling elements

   b) Traversing the DOM

   c) Attaching and retrieving custom data associated with an element

   d) Creating dynamic lists

8. Which jQuery method is used to handle keyboard events, such as keypress?

   a) `.click()`

   b) `.hover()`

   c) `.keypress()`
   d) `.submit()`
9. What does AJAX stand for in web development?
   a) Asynchronous JavaScript and XML
   b) Animated JavaScript and XHTML
   c) Advanced JSON and XML
   d) Asynchronous jQuery and XML
10. Which jQuery method is the core of jQuery's AJAX functionality?
   a) `$.get()`
   b) `$.post()`
   c) `$.getJSON()`
   d) `$.ajax()`

Answers

1. c) Web development
2. a) `.toggle()`
3. a) `.fadeToggle()`
4. b) `.after()`
5. b) Adds a class to an element
6. c) `.find()`
7. c) Attaching and retrieving custom data associated with an element
8. c) `.keypress()`
9. a) Asynchronous JavaScript and XML
10. d) `$.ajax()`

Index

Symbols

$.ajax() 159
$.get() 159
$.getJSON() 159
$.getScript() 159
$.post() 159
.after() 54
.animate() 40
.append() 50
.attr() 82
.before() 54
.click() 126
.clone() 55
.closest() 100
.fadeIn() 34
.fadeOut() 34
.fadeToggle() 35
.filter() 104
.find() 96
.get() 119
.height() 83
:hidden 105
.hide() 30
.hover() 126
.keypress() 126
.mousemove() method
  event object value,
    getting 140-143
  jQuery events
    listeners 137-139
  jQuery form,
    submitting 143, 145
.next() 101
.on() 126, 147, 148
.prepend() 50
.prev() 101
.preventDefault() 126, 152
.show() 31
.slideDown() 38
.slideToggle() 38

.slideUp() 37
.stopPropagation() 126, 147, 151
.submit() 126
.toggle() 34
.toggleClass() 85
.unwrap() 54
:visible 105
.width() 83
.wrap() 54

A

AJAX callback functions, types
  complete 169
  error 169
  success 168
AJAX external file, connecting 161-163
AJAX method
  about 162
  callback responses, handling 168, 169
AJAX method, callback options 163, 164
AJAX method, functions
  complete handler 163
  data 163
  datatype 163
  HTTP method 163
  other settings 163
  success, error handlers 163
  URL 163

C

CDN
  about 8
  benefits 8
  manipulating steps 9-12
child elements
  about 63
  manipulating 63
  selecting 63
Chrome Developer Tools
  application panel 13
  audits panel 13
  console 13
  device mode 13
  DevTools, accessing 13
  elements panel 13
  network panel 13
  performance panel 13
  setting, customizing 13
  sources panel 13
cloning elements
  about 64
  cloning 64
  exercise 65
  inserting 65
  modifying 65
content, elements adding
  button clicks, handling 52
  dynamic element, creating 53
  element, manipulating 52
  new page, creating 51
custom animations
  CSS, positioning 40
  exercise 43-46
  jQuery, using 40
custom animations CSS, properties
  margin 41
  position 41
  transform 41
  z- index 42, 43

D

data() 111
DOM elements
  Attribute selectors 19, 20
  basic selectors 17, 18
  filtering 23-25
  jQuery, using 17
  methods, chaining 26-28
  Pseudo selectors 20, 21
  traversal 21-23

E

element dimensions with jQuery
  getting 91, 93
element style, properties
  classes, toggling 86
  colors, generating 86
  output function 87
  testing 87
elements update, cloning
  elements clone, adding 56
  page with new content, replacing 55, 56
elements with jQuery
  elements, wrapping 54
  inserting 53
element with jQuery, manipulating
  content, changing 50
  element content, clearing 51
  element content, exploring 49, 50
  HTML content, modifying 50
  prepend, content appending 50
event bubbling
  about 151-153
  browsers, window events 153-156
event delegation 148
event Delegation 72
event, handling
  about 127
  jQuery event methods 128
  mouse events 134

F

Fading element
  jQuery, using 35-37
  Slide effect 38-40

G

getScript() 173

H

Hide, Show methods
  code breakdown 33, 34
  elements 32
HTML
  integration, verifying 7
  jQuery, adding 6
  jQuery, integrating 6, 7
  jQuery, obtaining 6
HTML classes, key point
  class attribute 60
  CSS, styling 60
HTML classes with jQuery, concepts
  classes, adding 60
  classes, removing 60, 61
  classes, understanding 60

I

index() 111, 116

J

jQuery
  about 1- 3
  callback options 168
  CDN 8
  Hide, Show methods 29-31
  history 2
  JSON data, getting 170
  user interactions, handling 2
  working 3, 4
jQuery attributes element
  setting up 87-91
jQuery, compelling reasons
  cross-browser compatibility 5
  curve, learning 5
  plugins ecosystem 5
  power embrace 5
  productivity, enhancing 5

jQuery CSS properties, determine
background color, changing 81
CSS, manipulating 81
CSS properties, changing 80
jQuery data method
data() 112
data, removing 113
data, retrieving 113
values, saving 112, 113
jQuery data method, exercise 114, 116
jQuery DOM manipulation, techniques
cloning elements 64
replace elements 66
wrapping elements 66
jQuery dynamic elements
modifying 62
new elements, creating 61, 62
removing 62
jQuery dynamic List
CSS, styling 72
HTML structure 72
interactivity 72
project overview 71
jQuery element attributes
manipulating 82
setting 82, 83
using 82
jQuery element dimensions
CSS classes, adding 83
CSS classes toggle 84, 85
layout adjustments 83
position, using 83
retrieving 83
width, height using 83
jQuery, elements
animation, effects 4
events, handling 4
jQuery elements, manipulating
child elements 63
parent elements 63
siblings 64
jQuery event methods
.click() method 128, 129
.hover() method 129, 131
.keypress() method 133, 134
.submit() method 131, 132
jQuery interactive
conclusion, outcomes learning 73
exercise 74-76
jQuery interactive, elements
dynamic updates 72
event listeners 72
user feedback 73
validation 73
jQuery interactivity, use methods
items, adding 72
items, removing 72
jQuery obtaining, ways
Content Delivery Network (CDN) 6
direct, downloading 6
jQuery page elements
ancestors, traversing 99, 100
descendants, finding 95
descendants, traversing 96-98
siblings other selections, traversing 101, 103
siblings, traversing 100, 101
state, visibilty 104-108
them, filtering 103, 104
jQuery shorthand method 167, 168 173

L

load() method 160
load() method, syntax
  complete 161
  data 161
  selector 161
  url 161

M

mouse events
  .hover() method 134
  .mousedown() method 135
  .mouseenter() method 137
  .mouseleave() method 136
  .mousemove() method 137
  .mouseout() method 135, 136
  .mouseover() method 136
  .mouseup() method 135

O

on method events,
    attaching 148-151

P

page element method
  element position 117-119
  .get() 119, 120
  index method 116, 117
  index value console 121-124
parent elements
  about 63
  selecting 63
  styling 63

R

replace elements
  about 66
  inserting 66
  replacing 66
  updating 66

S

selected element, inserting
  .insertAfter() 54
  .insertBefore() 54
selected element,
    techniques
  elements, cloning 55
  user interactions,
    inserting 55
siblings
  about 64
  selecting 64
  working 64

W

wrapping elements
  about 66
  exercise 67- 69
  removing 66
  reraining 67
  structure, optimizing 66